A Wee Guide to

St Margaret and
Malcolm Canmore

A WEE GUIDE TO

St Margaret and Malcolm Canmore

Charles Sinclair

GOBLINSHEAD
Musselburgh

Wee Guide to St Margaret and Malcolm Canmore

First Published 2003
© Martin Coventry 2003

Published by GOBLINSHEAD
130B Inveresk Road
Musselburgh EH21 7AY Scotland
tel 0131 665 2894; *fax* 0131 653 6566
email goblinshead@sol.co.uk

British Library Cataloguing in Publication Data
A catalogue record for this book is available from the British Library.

ISBN 1 899874 39 9

Typeset by GOBLINSHEAD using Desktop Publishing

If you would like a colour catalogue of our publications please contact the publishers at **Goblinshead, 130B Inveresk Road, Musselburgh EH21 7AY, Scotland, UK.**

Look out for other related Goblinshead titles (available from bookshops and other outlets, or directly from the publisher at the address above):

Wee Guide to Macbeth and Early Scotland (£3.95)

Wee Guide to William Wallace (£3.95)

Wee Guide to Robert the Bruce (£3.95)

Churches and Abbeys of Scotland (£5.95)

Contents

List of Illustrations

All photos, maps and family trees
by Martin Coventry, except for
The Landing of St Margaret at
Queensferry – mural by William
Hole (Scottish National Portrait
Gallery); Malcolm Canmore
(Bannerman) (Scottish National
Portrait Gallery); St Margaret's
Cave (19th century) (Fife Council
Museums); St Margaret's Head
Shrine (Abbot House Museum)
and St Margaret's Stone (Doug
Houghton).

Foreword

Margaret is one of the most popular, remarkable and beloved of women from Scotland's past, despite the fact that she died some 900 years ago. Her virtues and strengths as a woman, wife and queen were, and are, renowned, even at the beginning of the third millennium. Indeed, if anything her popularity has grown in recent times: more churches are now dedicated to Margaret than in medieval times.

Margaret is a saint whose virtues can be appreciated by people of modern times. Most female saints of her age were neither married nor mothers, and many were martyred for their faith. Margaret of Scotland, however, was happily married, had eight healthy children, and lived to a relatively ripe old age for the 11th century. She was content in her marriage, although she had an unruly husband and lived through difficult times, she loved her children (her ideas of discipline might be seen as somewhat strict for modern times!), she was charitable and generous with the poor and unfortunate, and she spent much of her day praying and at her devotions. She was also an eloquent and effective negotiator and had the power over her husband and his nobles to moderate, persuade and improve.

Malcolm Canmore seems to pale into insignificance in comparison to his saintly wife. He has been portrayed as little more than an ignorant savage who ruled a barbaric and backward nation. Yet this was far from the case. Malcolm Canmore was a shrewd and effective king, who recovered his realm from the strong and ruthless Macbeth, then maintained Scotland against the military power of William the Conqueror and the Normans when the whole of Saxon England was defeated. Malcolm had a long and successful reign, and left Scotland in a much better position than he had found it. Malcolm and Margaret's sons and heirs were then to shepherd Scotland through an age of relative peace and prosperity which lasted for nearly 200 years, a feat that neither those monarchs who went before, nor after, could achieve.

Margaret and Malcolm have rightly taken their place as two of foremost and most attractive characters from Scottish history.

C. S., Musselburgh, 2003

Acknowledgements

Thanks to everyone who helped with the book over the several years it has taken to get it to a point where it could be published – thanks to the many customers who have waited patiently.

Thanks particularly to Deborah Hunter at the National Gallery of Scotland, Lesley Botten at Fife Council Museums, to Abbot House in Dunfermline, and to Doug Houghton at Orkney Slide Library. Thanks also to Joyce Miller.

Photos, maps and family trees by Martin Coventry, except for:

Cover and frontispiece: The Landing of St Margaret at Queensferry – mural by William Hole (Scottish National Portrait Gallery)

Page 7: Malcolm Canmore (Bannerman)
(Scottish National Portrait Gallery)

Page 32: St Margaret's Cave (19th century)
(Fife Council Museums, Dunfermline Museum)

Page 48: St Margaret's Head Shrine
(Abbot House, Dunfermline)

Page 81: St Margaret's Stone
(Doug Houghton)

A WEE GUIDE TO

St Margaret and Malcolm Canmore

Calendar of Events

1005 Malcolm II becomes king of Scots.

1016 Edward the Exile (Margaret's father) forced into exile with Edward the Confessor when Cnut invades England.

1031? Birth of Malcolm Canmore, son of Duncan.

1037 Death of Cnut.

1040 Death of Malcolm II; Duncan, his grandson, is proclaimed king, then slain in battle by Macbeth. Malcolm Canmore flees to England.

1042 Edward the Confessor becomes King of England.

1046 Birth of Margaret in Hungary; she has a brother Edgar.

1053 Siward of Northumberland and Malcolm Canmore defeat Macbeth and Malcolm holds south of Scotland.

1054 Edward the Confessor summons Edward the Exile back to England.

1057 Macbeth slain at Lumphanan and Malcolm is confirmed as King of Scots and crowned at Scone; death of Edward the Exile.

1061 Malcolm raids Northumberland.

1066 Edward the Confessor dies and Harold becomes King of England. He is victorious at the Battle of Stamford Bridge but is slain by William the Conqueror at Hastings. The Normans invade England.

1067?, 1068? or 1070? Margaret and her brother Edgar flee to Scotland; Margaret marries Malcolm at Dunfermline. They have six sons – including the Scottish kings Edgar, Alexander I and David I – and two daughters.

1069 Edgar Atheling, Margaret's brother, seizes north of England but his forces are defeated by William the Conqueror.

1070 Malcolm raids Northumberland.

1072 William the Conqueror invades Scotland.

1079 Malcolm raids Northumberland.

1080 The English raid the south of Scotland.

1087 Death of William the Conqueror; William (II) Rufus, his son, becomes king.

1091 Edgar Atheling returns to Scotland, and Malcolm raids Northumberland. The Normans retaliate and Malcolm is forced to come to terms with William Rufus.

1092 William Rufus raids Scottish-held Cumbria.

1093 Malcolm raids into Northumberland in revenge but is slain, along with his son Edward, at Alnwick. Margaret is ill, and dies (16 November) at Edinburgh Castle soon after hearing of his death. Her body is taken to Dunfermline for burial. Malcolm is interred at Tynemouth, and his remains are not returned to Scotland for 20 years. Donald Bane proclaims himself king.

1094 Duncan II, Malcolm's eldest son by Ingioborg, defeats Donald Bane and becomes king. But Duncan is murdered, and Donald Bane regains the throne.

1097 Edgar (Margaret and Malcolm's son) deposes Donald Bane, and is proclaimed king. On his death, he is succeeded by Alexander, his brother.

1124 David I becomes king on the death of Alexander (his older brother).

1153 Malcolm IV the Maiden, grandson of David, becomes king.

1174 Accession of William the Lyon, brother of Malcolm IV.

1214 Alexander II, son of William, proclaimed king.

1249 Alexander III, son of Alexander II, becomes king

1250 After many miracles being attributed to her relics, Margaret is canonised by the Pope. Her remains are moved to a new relic chapel at Dunfermline.

1263 Battle of Largs: the Norwegians are defeated by the Scots fighting over the Western Isles.

1286 Death of Alexander III at Kinghorn.

1290 Death of Margaret, Maid of Norway, his granddaughter. There are no direct descendants. The Scots ask Edward I of England to mediate in the dispute, and he chooses John (John I) Balliol as king, first making him swear allegiance.

1296 John Balliol rebels against the English. Berwick is sacked and the Scots are defeated by Edward I of England at Dunbar. Scotland is invaded and so begins the Wars of Independence and centuries of fighting with the English.

1560- Margaret and Malcolm's relics are taken abroad following the Reformation and sacking of Dunfermline Abbey.

1603 James VI of Scots unites the kingdoms of Scotland and England.

Map 1: Margaret and Malcolm's Scotland

ORKNEY

● Stronsay

● Kirkwall

● St Margaret's Hope

WESTERN
ISLES

SKYE

Spynie ● ● Urquhart
M o r a y Strathbogie ● ● Forgue
Inverness ● ● King's Haugh
Lumphanan ● Aberdeen ●

Pictland
● Cowie
● Laurencekirk
● Brechin
● Clunie ● Forfar
Dunkeld ● ● Kinclaven ● Arbroath
● Dunsinane
Perth ● Scone
Auchterarder ● ● ● Abernethy ● St Andrews
Loch Leven ● Abercrombie
Stirling ● Dunfermline ● Kinghorn FORTH
St Margaret's Hope ● ● ● Inchcolm ● Dunbar
Dumbarton ● Falkirk ● Queensferry *Lothian*
Edinburgh ●
Berwick ●
Melrose ● ● Kelso ●
Dryburgh ● Carham
Jedburgh ●

MULL
● Kerrera
● Iona
Argyll
Dalriada

● Largs

CLYDE

S t r a t h c l y d e

Galloway

Northumberland
ENGLAND

● Carlisle

Cumbria

Introduction

By the 11th century the kingdom of Scots was well established, the two realms of Pictland and Dalriada having been united by Kenneth MacAlpin in 834. He moved from his power base in the west, partly as a response to increased attacks by Vikings. In the following centuries the kingdom was consolidated, incorporating Strathclyde and Lothian. This was not a peaceful time, however, with continued strife both from within the borders of Scotland and from without. Kings would ascend to the throne, but most were quickly deposed by rivals or were killed in battle, uprisings or raids.

So it was that Kenneth's descendant, the young Duncan, came to the throne in 1034. He, like many of his predecessors, was not to reign long, and was slain in battle by Macbeth, although not in his bed with a bloody dagger as described by Shakespeare. Macbeth, despite what is said about him in the famous Scottish play, ruled well and long for the times, and even made a pilgrimage to Rome in 1050.

In 1053, however, Macbeth was defeated in battle, possibly at Dunsinane or at Scone in Perthshire, and four years later was killed at Lumphanan in Deeside by the forces of Malcolm Canmore, Malcolm III, King of Scots.

Malcolm Canmore, Duncan's son, had been sheltered in England, and he only defeated Macbeth with English aid. Canmore means big head or big leader, and he was named King of Scots. More memorably perhaps, Malcolm was to marry one of the most remarkable women of these days, and one of the most famous women in Scottish history.

Margaret was from the Saxon royal family of England, which was forced into exile when the Vikings seized England. Having returned to England, Margaret then had to flee to Scotland along with her brother Edgar Atheling, the Saxon heir of England, when the Norman William the Conqueror invaded Scotland's southern neighbour. Malcolm Canmore and Margaret were married, and are believed to have been happy together, having eight children, four of whom would become kings of Scots and one a queen of England. Margaret was revered for her piety and good works, and after her death miracles were attributed to her relics. In 1250 she was canonised by the Pope.

Unlike most women of the medieval period, a lot was known about Margaret, or at least was written about her. *The Life of Queen Margaret* was compiled by her confessor, Turgot, although how much was augmented in later centuries is not clear. Many of the historical events are also recorded in several 'contemporary' sources, including the *Anglo-Saxon Chronicle* and the *Chronicon of Florence of Worcester*.

The marriage of Margaret and Malcolm has been portrayed almost as a union between beauty and the beast, between Mother Teresa and Conan the Barbarian. The reality seems to be Margaret was far more worldly than some would later record, and Malcolm was not as barbaric as reports made him, being no better or worse than his contemporaries.

The lives of Margaret and Malcolm Canmore, their sons and descendants, form a memorable tale, a dynasty of effective monarchs in an age of relative peace and prosperity for Scotland, while the rest of Britain was often rent by warfare.

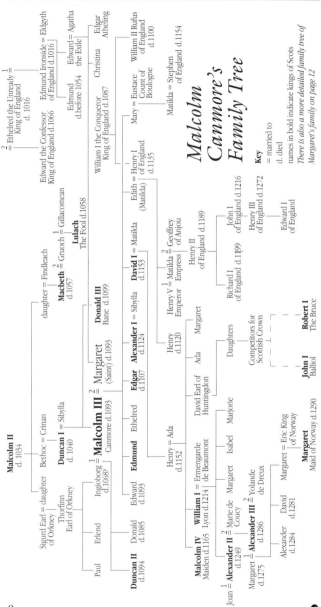

Malcolm Canmore's Family Tree

Key
= married to
d. died
names in bold indicate kings of Scots
There is also a more detailed family tree of Margaret's family on page 12

Margaret and Malcolm Canmore

Margaret and Malcolm Canmore were to become two of the most influential people in Britain in the second half of the 11th century. But it could have been very different. Malcolm was the son of Duncan (more famous from his murder in the play by Shakespeare than anything he himself was to achieve in real life). Duncan was slain in battle with Macbeth, who then became King of Scots. Malcolm had to flee from Scotland and seek refuge in England. He was to have a strong, effective and certainly ruthless enemy in Macbeth.

Margaret's family, from the Saxon royal house of England, was also to lose its kingdom, but to the Norsemen under the powerful Cnut, more commonly known as Canute, and famous for trying to prevent the tide from coming in (it was actually to show that men, even kings, had only limited power and could not control God's creation). Margaret was born in Hungary after her family were banished from England. Although they were to return, they were then to face a new threat from the Normans.

It is necessary to go back to the beginning of the 11th century to understand the lives of Margaret and Malcolm.

In 1005 Malcolm II became King of Scots: he was the great-grandfather of Malcolm Canmore, who was to become Malcolm III. Malcolm II was to rule a divided kingdom which was under attack from within and without, most especially from the Vikings. The Norsemen raided the coasts, and later had come as settlers, creating the powerful Earldom of Orkney, and controlling the islands around Scotland and parts of the northern mainland. Malcolm had no surviving sons, but had a grandson Duncan, through his daughter Bethoc, who in turn had a son, Malcolm Canmore, around 1031.

Scotland at that time was divided into several kingdoms and areas. Malcolm II controlled the lands north of the Forth and Clyde, while Lothian was controlled by Northumberland, and Strathclyde by its own kings. Orkney, Shetland and the Western Isles were held by the Norsemen.

The kingdom of Scots had been weakened by dynastic quarrels and infighting. Succession by the firstborn had not been established, and kings were 'chosen' from suitable male heirs. Consequently, a brother was more likely to become king than a son. This did mean that any strong and ruthless individual from within the royal house could become king. The throne could be acquired (although not always secured) by killing rivals, securing powerful allies often from outwith the borders of the kingdom, and – of course – by backing from a strong army.

Malcolm II was an able ruler. First he turned on enemies within the kingdom, and secured his borders against the Vikings. Then he led an army against the kingdom of Northumberland, and won the Battle of Carham in 1018. The victory secured Lothian as part of his kingdom. Owen the Bald, the King of Strathclyde, who was allied with the Scots, was killed at the battle, and the ancient kingdom of Strathclyde was absorbed into the kingdom of Scots.

The kingdom now had the southern border more

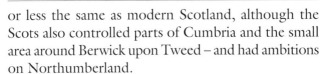

or less the same as modern Scotland, although the Scots also controlled parts of Cumbria and the small area around Berwick upon Tweed – and had ambitions on Northumberland.

Malcolm II died in 1040 and his grandson Duncan (Malcolm Canmore's father), preferred by his grandfather, was proclaimed king. He was both young and ineffective, first losing a battle against the Norsemen under Thorfinn the Mighty (his cousin), the Earl of Orkney, then engaging Macbeth (probably another cousin), who Duncan may have regarded as a dangerous rival. Duncan was defeated near Spynie in Moray, and was mortally wounded during the battle to die soon after the fight. Macbeth and Thorfinn may have been allies.

Malcolm Canmore was about 10 ten years of age and had no choice but to flee south. He was sheltered in England, and spent his next years protected in Northumberland by Earl Siward, his uncle through his mother, and then later also at the court of Edward the Confessor, King of England.

Macbeth was to prove an able ruler and was no doubt as godly as his contemporaries – he felt sufficiently secure to be able to go on pilgrimage to Rome, where he distributed money to the poor 'like seed'. His wife also had a name, Gruoch. They did not have any children, but Gruoch had a son by a previous marriage, Lulach, who had a claim to the throne through his mother.

Meanwhile, England, too, was under threat from the Vikings. In 1016 Ethelred II (the Unready), King of England, died and, later that year, so did Edmund

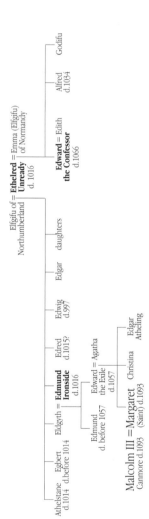

Margaret's Family Tree

Key

= married to

d. died

names in bold indicate kings of England

There is also a family tree of Malcolm Canmore on page 8

Ironside. Following his death, England was seized by the Vikings, and ruled by the famous Cnut (also known as Canute, as mentioned above) after he had been victorious at Ashingdon in Essex. Edmund's sons were forced into exile after his death, along with their uncle Edward, later King of England and known as the Confessor. Edmund's sons, another Edmund (who died in Hungary) and Edward the Exile, fled to the continent and found shelter with the devout King Stephen of Hungary (who died in 1038), then his successor King Andrew. Stephen's court was as magnificent as any in Europe, and Stephen was renowned for his piety, being canonised shortly after his death.

Cnut was a great man himself, and became King of Denmark, on the death of his brother Harold in 1019. Although he lost a sea battle against the kings of Sweden and Norway, and lost Denmark temporarily, he later added Norway to his possessions. Cnut was as pious as his contemporaries and also went on pilgrimage to Rome.

In 1037 Cnut died, and Harold Harefoot, his son, was made Regent of England. Five years later Harold died, and after the brief two-year rule of Harthacnut, another son of Cnut, Edward the Confessor was eventually inaugurated as King of England.

Margaret was born at Castle Reka in southern Hungary in 1046. Her father, Edward the Exile, did not return to England after the accession of her uncle Edward the Confessor.

The following year William (later known as the Conqueror) was acknowledged as the Norman Duke of Normandy.

In 1053 Malcolm was old enough to try to recover his father's throne, and with English help (Edward the Confessor supported the removal of Macbeth) and an army, under Siward, Earl of Northumberland, he marched north. Malcolm (or Siward, anyway) brought Macbeth to battle, traditionally at Dunsinane Hill, near Perth, although Scone has also been suggested as the location for the fighting. Although Macbeth was defeated and many of his best men apparently slain, he survived the battle and fled north, securing the north part of Scotland as his realm.

Malcolm and the English do not appear to have been strong enough to continue the fight north (Siward's son and nephew were slain): it is possible that the battle was sufficiently bloody to weaken them or, alternatively, that the English army was bloated with plunder and wanted to return home with their loot. It is interesting that Siward robbed and pillaged widely and at will, but this is not held against him; while Malcolm Canmore's later raids into Northumberland are widely condemned. Incidentally, Norman mercenaries fought for Macbeth, although they left Scotland after his defeat.

Whatever the truth of it, Macbeth continued to rule the north for another four years. Macbeth and Gruoch had no children, however, although Lulach, Gruoch's son and Macbeth's stepson, had a claim to the throne through her.

In 1055 Siward died, and Malcolm Canmore was powerful enough to continue the battle against Macbeth alone. Then two years later Macbeth was waylaid by Malcolm's forces at Lumphanan in

Scone Palace – Malcolm Canmore was inaugurated as King of Scots at Scone on the death of Macbeth.

Aberdeenshire, and was slain. Lulach was put up as king by Macbeth's supporters but he was killed the following year.

Malcolm Canmore became king of the whole of the kingdom of Scots, and was inaugurated on the famous Stone of Destiny (also known as the Stone of Scone and now housed in Edinburgh Castle) at Scone, near Perth, on 25 April. Malcolm was the third king of that name to rule the kingdom of Scots, and is known as Canmore. This may have been an acknowledgement of his overlordship (from the Gaelic *Ceann Mor*: big head or big chief), but it may have been purely descriptive and Malcolm may simply have had a large head.

Although he was married to Edith, daughter of Godwine, Earl of Wessex, Edward the Confessor had no children (nor was he likely to) and it was not clear who was to be next in line to the English throne. It was decided that it would be prudent to decide on an heir while the Confessor was still alive, to avoid any confusion which their enemies could exploit when he died (which is what had happened with the death of Edmund Ironside). The influence of the Normans had been growing in England: Elfgifu, sister of Richard II, Duke of Normandy, was the second wife of Ethelred. It is possible that in 1051 the kingdom was offered to William, Duke of Normandy, during a visit to England – he was certainly to claim that it had been.

This would hardly have been to the liking of the Saxons. In 1054 Margaret's father Edward the Exile was summoned back to England so that he might be considered as a possible future king, but Edward had not long returned to England in 1057 when he died. The *Anglo-Saxon Chronicle* lamented the death of this good man as a 'misfortune of this wretched people' (meaning the English). Edgar, Edward's son, was now a possible candidate for the throne, and so was known as the 'Atheling', meaning that he was the chosen heir. He was, however, young and may have been physically weak, and Edward the Confessor was known to prefer Harold. This left the succession open again, although Margaret and her family remained in England.

Malcolm's Reign

In 1058 Lulach (usually known as 'the Fool'), had been put forward as the King of Scots, but Malcolm Canmore arranged to have him slain at Essie in Strathbogie. Lulach had a son, Maelsnectai, but he (probably wisely) placed himself in a monastery. Lulach's descendants, through a daughter, became rulers of Moray.

Malcolm married Ingioborg in 1059 or so. She was probably the daughter (although it has been suggested that she might have been the widow) of Thorfinn the Mighty, the Norse Earl of Orkney. They had two sons, Duncan (later Duncan II) and Donald, who died before his father in 1085; and possibly a third son. Ingioborg probably died around 1068, although no specific mention is made of this in the records of the time. This union with a Norse princess helped secure Malcolm's northern lands and counter the threat from the Vikings.

Malcolm was sufficiently confident in his rule that he made a raid into Northumberland in 1061, perhaps pursuing his own claim to the Earldom. The new Earl of Northumberland, Tostig (who was the future King Harold's brother), was on pilgrimage at the time, so it was an opportune chance to attack, even though Malcolm and Tostig are said to have had a bond of mutual friendship. This was a reputedly fearsome raid, and even the holy island of Lindisfarne was sacked. It is questionable whether this was any more fearsome than Siward's looting of Scotland following the battle against Macbeth.

Malcolm has often been criticised for this raid, and

the others to follow, and no particular reason is given why he should have attacked an area which had given him support in the fight against Macbeth. It should be noted, however, that these raids were far less damaging than the slaughter and destruction wrought in Yorkshire and elsewhere by William the Conqueror. Raiding and fighting were expected of kings of these times, and were an essential means of supplementing wealth through the acquisition of gold, silver, cattle and even slaves. It made no sense to so devastate an area that it could not recover quickly. Anyway, this was a turbulent and violent age, and Malcolm was a king of his time.

Edward the Confessor died in January 1066, and Harold of Wessex, son of Earl Godwine, was chosen as his successor, not Margaret's brother Edgar.

Malcolm Canmore, perhaps because of his marriage to Ingioborg or perhaps because he wanted to extend his influence south into Northumberland, supported the Vikings under Harold Hardrada, King of Norway, and Tostig when they attacked the north of England. Tostig was King Harold of England's brother, although after many misdeeds he had been replaced as the Earl of Northumberland in 1065 and was then banished from England. This alliance of Vikings and Northumbrians won a battle against the local earls, and seized York. Harold, King of England, had many problems in 1066, not least William of Normandy threatening to invade England from France. Harold's northern enemies had seized their chance, and struck when the English king's attention was elsewhere.

Harold hurried north with his army, and the Vikings

and Northumbrians were crushed in September at the Battle of Stamford Bridge. Both Harold Hardrada and Tostig were slain. It might have gone ill for Malcolm had Harold not had other concerns, but at that point William, Duke of Normandy, was invading England from France, landing on 29 September at Pevensey on the south coast. Harold had to hurry south to meet this new threat.

Harold and the English met William and the Normans at Hastings on 14 October in the south of England, and he was defeated and slain at the battle, having been shot in the eye with an arrow. The Normans under William invaded the now defenceless country. William the Conqueror was made King of England on Christmas Day 1066.

Margaret and her family remained in England, although her brother was the focus for the Anglo-Saxons in the north and the midlands. It was feared that they would be imprisoned or worse, and the family, along with many Northumbrian nobles, eventually decided to flee.

Margaret and Edgar Atheling took ship, with their mother Agatha and sister Christina (the latter who was also a goodly and pious lass, although somewhat strict for modern tastes, and was to enter a convent). They made land in Fife in Scotland, at the bay now called St Margaret's Hope, just south of Rosyth on the north bank of the Forth and just a few miles south of Malcolm Canmore's palace at Dunfermline.

It is not clear whether they intended to seek sanctuary in Scotland with Malcolm Canmore, although it is likely. Malcolm was gladly receiving all English fugitives and placing them under his protection. Edgar may have seen Scotland as a good base from which to recover his kingdom of England. It has been suggested, however, that their vessel may have been caught in a storm and blown off course, and they were actually seeking passage to the Continent and renewed exile in Hungary.

Malcolm may have already met Margaret at the court of Edward the Confessor in England or in Northumberland after the Norman invasion. Whatever other motive he may have had, the advantage of a match between the Saxon heirs of England and the kings of Scots would have been obvious to Malcolm, and he hurried from Dunfermline to meet Edgar and his sister. It does also appear that Margaret was a very attractive young woman.

It is clear however, at least initially, that she yearned for a monastic life in a nunnery, and desired to be only the bride of Christ. It is also recorded that Edgar was not in favour of the match, and was forced into agreement as he was in the protection and power of the Scottish king. The *Anglo Saxon Chronicle* records that she agreed to the match so that she could direct Malcolm from his erring ways, increase God's praise in the land, and suppress the evil customs which the people had formerly used. In other words, her holy mission was to redeem Scotland and its king from their rough and ready ways.

Whether it was a politically convenient and attractive match for Malcolm and a wedding forced on Margaret, who then decided to make the best of a bad lot by improving her husband and kingdom; or whether the couple fell deeply in love from the outset,

The scant but massive remains of Malcolm's Tower, Pittencrieff Park – Malcolm and Margaret are said to have been married here.

the outcome was that Malcolm Canmore married Margaret. The exact year is not known, as sources of the time give different dates: 1067, 1068 or 1070. The couple are said to have been married at the site of Malcolm's Tower, the reduced ruin of which stands in Pittencrieff Park in Dunfermline, but it may have been at what was to become Dunfermline Abbey.

Although Malcolm attempted to conceal the wedding from his southern neighbour, it greatly angered William the Conqueror, who rightly feared a union between the Saxons and Scots. William's position as king of England was still precarious, and it must have been a hard blow to find that the Scots and the Saxons were uniting against him, and that Malcolm was encouraging English fugitives.

In 1069 Edgar Atheling, aided by Cospatric, Earl of Yorkshire, tried to stop the northern spread of the

Normans and Durham was seized and widespread rebellion followed. Edgar got help from the King of Denmark, but when William arrived in the north with a large army, the Danes withdrew (they may have been paid off). The rising failed, Yorkshire was ravaged, and William was now master of all the lands to the Tweed, the border with the kingdom of Scots.

In 1070 it was left to Malcolm Canmore to attack Northumberland through his own lands in Cumbria. William had been planting his own people in the area, and Malcolm plundered the earldom between the Tees and the Tyne, although he failed to take the strategically important fortress of Bamburgh.

The purpose of Malcolm's raid may have been to pursue the claim of his brother-in-law Edgar to the English throne, but it is likely he wished to make Northumberland part of his own realm, a policy which was successful, albeit temporarily, under his son

Bamburgh Castle, Northumberland – Malcolm Canmore failed to take Bamburgh when he raided the earldom in 1070.

David I. It may also be that he feared the strength of the Normans, and was making a pre-emptive strike to stop them overwhelming Cumbria and Lothian.

This attack is recorded as being especially punitive, and it is said that as a result virtually every household in southern Scotland had English slaves. The devastation is likely to have been exaggerated or it would not have been worth Malcolm's time raiding the earldom three more times in the following years. William the Conqueror's own devastation in Yorkshire was such that it took generations to restore just some of the prosperity of the area.

All was to change when Hereward the Wake, the last major Saxon threat to his power, was defeated by William in 1070. William was now eager to deal with his turbulent northern neighbour, being angered both by the ravaging of Northumberland, and Malcolm's support for Edgar Atheling.

William crossed the border and invaded Scotland in 1072, supported by a large fleet. Malcolm chose not to meet him in battle, and he paid homage to William (or at least agreed to the woolly phrase that he would become William's man) at Abernethy near Perth. Wisely for both men, perhaps, war was avoided, and Malcolm shrewdly bargained with the Normans. Malcolm's son Duncan was taken as a hostage to ensure Malcolm's co-operation. Encouraged by Malcolm, Edgar Atheling eventually made his peace with William, and was given lands in Normandy.

In 1077, Maelsnectai, son of Lulach the Fool, led a rising in the large province of Moray, but this was quickly put down by Malcolm.

Dunfermline Abbey Church – Malcolm and Margaret founded a church here, dedicated to The Holy Trinity, in about 1070.

William the Conqueror was busy with troubles in France when Malcolm raided into Northumberland around the middle of August 1079, causing mayhem between the Tweed and the Tyne, then retreating north. It is recorded that he slew many hundreds of men, and carried off much treasure and precious things.

In retaliation, the following year the Normans, under Robert, son of William the Conqueror, raided deep into the south of Scotland, getting all the way to the River Carron near Falkirk. Again the Scots retreated without fighting, and eventually the English withdrew. Castles, however, were built at Newcastle upon Tyne and at Carlisle to defend against Scottish incursions.

William the Conqueror died in France on 9 September 1087, and William (II) Rufus, his son, became king.

In 1091 Edgar Atheling returned to Scotland, having been dispossessed of his lands in Normandy by the new king. William Rufus was out of England in France. Malcolm used this as a pretext and raided into Northumberland again, apparently insulted that the new English king had not received him at court.

This time the English retaliated in strength and Malcolm was forced come to terms, although again he avoided battle. It appears Malcolm recognised William Rufus as his feudal superior, but William confirmed the lands already in the possession of the Scots, including Malcolm's lands in Cumbria. It is not clear whether this superiority was only acknowledged for the lands in Cumbria in England or for the whole of Scotland.

The understanding was short lived. In 1092 William Rufus raided the parts of Cumbria held by Malcolm Canmore, strengthening the garrison of Carlisle Castle, and planting friends or followers in the area.

The Making of A Saint

Margaret was born around 1046 in Castle Reka in southern Hungary, and was the granddaughter of Edmund Ironside, King of England, and also the niece of Edward the Confessor, the future and godly king of England. Her father, Edward the Exile, had been banished from England and fled to the Continent in 1042 and the protection of King Stephen (later Saint) of Hungary.

Margaret's mother was Agatha, probably the daughter of King Stephen of Hungary or a cousin of Gisela, Stephen's queen. Margaret had two siblings: a brother Edgar, and Christina, her sister, who was destined to spend her life in convents. The court of Stephen, and then Andrew, was a very religious place, and a wave of piety was sweeping through Europe since the world had not ended at the turn of the millennium: a wave which swept Margaret and her family along.

Edward the Exile was asked to return to England in 1054 when Margaret was about nine years of age, but the Exile did not long survive his arrival in 1057. When Edward the Confessor finally died in 1066, Margaret's brother, Edgar, was passed over in the succession for Harold, but Margaret and her family remained in England. Harold was soon slain at the Battle of Hastings when William the Conqueror and the Normans invaded. Edgar, as the Saxon heir to the throne of England, found it prudent to remove himself and his family from England after the tide of wars had gone against him

Margaret seems to have been a very attractive girl,

Dunfermline Abbey – the nave of the present building dates from the reign of Margaret and Malcolm's son David I.

and was in her twenties when she had to flee from England with Edgar, Agatha, Christina and other notable Northumbrians. They landed at St Margaret's Hope, near Rosyth, and Malcolm hurried from Dunfermline to meet them. He may have fallen in love with Margaret, although the marriage was also politically convenient for him. The couple appear to have been as happy as any royal couple of the time. Much has also been made of the difference in Margaret's and Malcolm's ages, but in medieval times this would have not been thought unusual. Margaret was in her twenties, Malcolm a hale and hearty forty or so (although he was to remain sufficiently fit to be raiding England into his sixties), and they were to be married for more than twenty years. They were married at Dunfermline.

Margaret and Malcolm were to have six sons, the eldest called Edward, and two daughters. Their children were given English, rather than Gaelic, names. Four of their sons – Edmund, Edgar, Alexander and David – were to become kings of Scots (although Edmund, the oldest of these four, only very briefly), while Ethelred, another son, was Abbot of Dunkeld, and died relatively young. Edith, the older daughter, and called Matilda or Maud by the Normans (who could not pronounce Edith), married Henry V, Holy Roman Emperor, then Henry I of England. Henry was the son of William the Conqueror, and this united the Saxon and Norman lines of descent to the English throne: Henry II of England was Margaret and Malcolm's great grandson. The younger daughter, Mary, was to marry Eustace, Count of Boulogne, and their daughter, also known as Maud, married Stephen of Mortain, King of England.

Margaret certainly was, it is recorded, a very pious, devout and charitable woman, and appears to have exerted a considerable influence over her husband. She did much good work, such as caring for, feeding and clothing the destitute, widows and orphans, said to number as many as 300 people at one time. Some 24 poor folk were looked after by her at all times, and she would herself feed orphaned babies from her knee.

She is even said to have stolen newly minted gold coins to give to the poor, encouraging Malcolm and others of the nobility to donate their wealth and belongings. It should be said that Malcolm was also noted for his piety, although presumably only when he was not raiding and plundering Northumberland. Margaret is credited with having many English slaves freed.

Malcolm (or Margaret) is said to have built a church dedicated to The Trinity not far from his residence at Dunfermline (perhaps because they had been married there, perhaps there was already a church on the site), and Margaret decided to found a monastery, inviting a small party of Benedictine monks, only three in total, from Canterbury.

Dunfermline was to become one of the most important abbeys in Scotland. In Margaret's time,

Iona Abbey – Margaret revived the monastery here and may have had St Oran's Chapel (to the left of the photo) built.

however, it was small, and it would not be until the reign of David I that the great abbey church was built. The foundations of an earlier church were found at the abbey, and are marked out in floor of the present nave. Margaret is said to have endowed the church with altar ornaments of gold and silver.

St Margaret's Stone, between North Queensferry and Dunfermline Abbey, is said to be where she rested on journeys to Dunfermline, and where ordinary people came to her to find help. Margaret became associated with fertility, as she had so many successful pregnancies, and this stone was visited by women who wished to conceive. Her shirt or sark was also worn by several queens, both to conceive and to achieve a successful birth, including by Mary of Gueldres when giving birth to the future James III, and Margaret Tudor for the future James V. Incidentally, St Margaret of Antioch is the patron saint of women, and is also associated with childbirth.

Margaret revived the monastery on Iona, which had suffered since the area had become controlled by the Vikings. She is credited with having St Oran's Chapel (later the burial place of the Lords of the Isles) built or rebuilt there, and with restoring the other buildings and providing money for the monks. Malcolm and Margaret may have even visited the island, although this seems unlikely. Iona had been the traditional burial place of the monarchs of Scotland, but Dunfermline was to replace it as such. Iona and the Western Isles were soon to fall firmly into the grasp of the Norsemen, and would not be recovered until 1266.

The church of St Rule at St Andrews, the tower of which survives, may have also been built at her instigation: it dates from as early as 1070. She certainly donated the image of a crucifix to St Andrews, as well as endowing other churches. Margaret provided shelter and food for pilgrims. She founded a free ferry, providing ships for the purpose, across the narrowest part of the Forth for pilgrims, both

St Rule's Church – dating from as early as 1070, stands by the ruins of the cathedral.

Scots and English, on their way to St Andrews (between what is now North and South Queensferry). She also founded hostels where they could shelter on their travels. Those who were not pilgrims had to pay for the ferry, even the Bishop of St Andrews.

Presumably much of Margaret's largesse was paid for by Malcolm's raids into Northumberland.

Margaret spent much of her day at personal devotions, attending services, praying, reading sacred texts, and singing psalms, and she often fasted: Turgot records that she did not eat for pleasure, only to sustain life, and that she suffered acute pain in her stomach for

St Margaret's Cave, Dunfermline c.1900 – Margaret's retreat near the abbey, where she came to pray and contemplate.

the rest of her life. The fact that she was to have eight healthy children suggests, however, that she herself was well nourished. The pain from which she suffered may have been a result of carrying and delivering eight babies rather than from fasting. Margaret found a retreat at what is now known as St Margaret's Cave, near Dunfermline Abbey. The cave is accessible, although it now lies under a car park.

Margaret greatly cherished her gospel book, which was encrusted with gold and jewels (and which Malcolm reputedly repeatedly kissed in homage to her learning and goodness – Malcolm could not read). She managed to lose the book crossing a ford, but when it was found in the water it was found to be undamaged except for a few stained pages. Turgot suggests that this was a miracle. The gospel book was taken from Scotland and is now held in the Bodleian Library in Oxford (there is a copy on display at St

Margaret's Chapel), it was purchased in 1887 for £6. There are water marks on some of the back pages.

Turgot records that Margaret was strict with her children, and she believed that 'he who spares the rod hates his son'. It is said that they were very well mannered and respectful, and her sons would go on to found many abbeys themselves. She sent her two daughters to England, where they were instructed at Romsey Priory by Margaret's sister Christina, who was nun there from 1086. Edith escaped from the convent in her teenage years, and she does not appear to have had a good relationship with her aunt.

It may have been in Hungary that Margaret acquired the famous relic which became known as the Black Rood of Scotland, a casket believed to contain a piece of the true cross on which Christ was crucified. The casket was made of gold and had an ebony crucifix emblazoned on the outside. The Black Rood was very famous, and Margaret held it as she died. It was presented to Holyrood Abbey, by what is now Holyroodhouse, by David I (Margaret's son), but was stolen from Scotland by Edward I of England, along with other relics, treasures and state documents. The Black Rood was recovered in 1328, only to be lost again by David II at the Battle of Neville's Cross in 1346. It was taken from the Scots and preserved at Durham Cathedral in the north of England, only to be lost, presumably destroyed, at the Reformation.

Margaret went on pilgrimage herself, although in some cases only men were apparently allowed to visit shrines. Margaret attempted to visit the shrine of St Laurence, probably at Laurencekirk in the Mearns,

St Margaret's gospel book – a copy is on display at St Margaret's Chapel at Edinburgh Castle, while the original is in the Bodleian Library in Oxford.

only to find that she was prevented from entering the church by divine intervention – or so it would appear. She was rendered unconscious, and only recovered after prayers were said over her. It does seem ironic that Malcolm the Barbarian could have visited without problem, while his pious wife was prevented from doing so. Margaret, however, gave a cross and chalice to the church, and is said to have prayed to St Laurence. It is interesting that Margaret was to go on to become a much more famous and venerated saint than Laurence, at least in Scotland.

Margaret is also recorded as being associated with St Catherine's Balm Well at Liberton on the outskirts of Edinburgh. One story is that the well sprang from a drop of holy oil which was being transported from the Holy Land to Margaret. The well was dedicated to St Catherine of Alexandria, who was martyred around 310 by beheading (milk rather than blood ran from the wound), although she is more famous for the Catherine Wheel. Catherine was determined to convert many Romans to Christianity, and the emperor tried to have her broken on a spiked wheel, but the wheel exploded without injuring her: he then had her beheaded. Her cult swept across Europe. The balm (or oily) well was believed to be a healing well, and effective for eczema, a painful and crusting condition of the skin, and possibly leprosy. The waters were still being used in 1910.

Margaret is also often credited with (or accused of) asserting the ways of the English or Roman church over those of the Celtic church, and hastening, if not precipitating, the demise of the latter. There is, however, little evidence for this claim. She respected or even admired the Culdees (a strict and austere group of 'Celtic' monks who lived in isolated communities devoted to God) and many of the traditional beliefs of the Scottish church of the time; the church, itself, seems to have already been stagnant, and perhaps even in decline. Indeed, Malcolm and Margaret supported Culdee communities, confirming a grant of land to the Culdees of Loch Leven.

The Scottish church, as had the churches in Ireland and Wales, had developed in its own fashion since Christianity was introduced to Scotland in the first half of the 5th century. Margaret encouraged the Scots, who had strayed somewhat from what was seen as 'orthodox' or mainstream practice, to fall into line with the church in Rome in the calculation of beginning of Lent, not working on Sundays, standardising how Mass was celebrated throughout the country, and the forbidding of marriage in circumstances such as between widows and brother-in-laws and step-parents and children.

This, however, was done with reasoned argument at a three day gathering. Malcolm acted as her interpreter (Margaret did not learn Gaelic), and the clerics agreed with Margaret, such was the wisdom of her words. What Malcolm actually said to them is not recorded, but such 'illegal' practices are said to have been completely eradicated.

There does not appear to have been any opposition to these changes, and it may be that Turgot overemphasised exactly what was achieved, and these changes to worship were quite minor or unimportant to those involved. It is also difficult to see in a country as disorderly as the Scotland of the time, with no direct central control, how it could be confirmed whether her wishes had been implemented or not. It was rather David I, who came to the throne in 1124, who was responsible for creating a strong centralised church which looked to Rome, with the building of many abbeys and the setting up or restoration of cathedrals, dioceses and parishes.

Margaret is also charged with forcing English or European customs and culture on to her Scottish subjects: as mentioned above she did not learn to speak Gaelic, although this was the tongue of the Scottish court (luckily Malcolm was fluent in English and Gaelic). Malcolm, it should be remembered however, had also spent many of his formative years in England, and the customs and culture may not have been alien to him or others at his court. He may have made many of these changes, if changes they were, without the

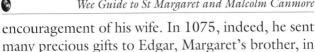

encouragement of his wife. In 1075, indeed, he sent many precious gifts to Edgar, Margaret's brother, in France.

Margaret is certainly credited with smartening up the Scottish nobility and court, and with introducing gold and silver plate for meals and hangings for the walls, many of which were embroidered by her or her ladies. It should be said, however, that there was much bias against the Scots by their English neighbours, and those who recorded the events were not Scots, nor sympathetic towards them, regarding them little better than ignorant savages. It might be claimed that their portrayal of the barbarism of the Scots was somewhat exaggerated.

As mentioned above, Margaret and Malcolm were married at Dunfermline, and Malcolm certainly had a palace or residence there, traditionally at the ruinous tower, known as Malcolm's Tower, in Pittencrieff Park in the town. The ruins of this tower, however, likely date from no earlier that the 13th or 14th century. Indeed, there are no certain remains dating from the 11th century. Malcolm is believed, however, to have had palaces or strongholds at Dunfermline (as above), at Edinburgh Castle, Stirling Castle, Forfar, Aberdeen and Inverness, as well as at Auchterarder, Clunie and Kinclaven near Blairgowrie, Cowie near Stonehaven, and King's Haugh near Dufftown.

Margaret and Malcolm's Deaths

In 1093 Malcolm responded to the ravaging of his lands in Cumbria by leading a further raid into England. He broke into Northumberland, and rode towards Alnwick, accompanied by a large force including his sons, apparently meaning to waste the earldom and take revenge on Rufus's supporters.

Margaret was seriously ill: she had not been able to ride a horse and had seldom risen from her bed for at least six months, possibly a result of numerous births, or perhaps through too much fasting. She begged Malcolm not to go. Some days later she told those around her that evil had befallen the kingdom of Scots.

Her fears were to prove well founded. Malcolm was treacherously murdered, along with his eldest son Edward, when accepting the surrender of Alnwick

Alnwick Castle, Northumberland – Malcolm Canmore was slain near here after he had been promised the castle would surrender.

Castle. He is said to have been betrayed by a trusted companion: a lance with the keys of the castle were thrust through his eye. The other men with him were also slain, although at least some must have escaped, including his son Edgar. It is possible Malcolm had only a small force with him, while the rest of his army was nearby. A cross near Alnwick Castle marks the reputed spot where they were slain.

Margaret had not recovered, and was waiting for any news of her husband. Edgar, their son, hurried north and reached Edinburgh four days later, finding his mother in her sick bed. Margaret had the double blow of losing both her husband and eldest son, and she was stricken, perhaps even praying that she might be allowed to die, according to the *Anglo-Saxon Chronicle*.

She received the news with the Black Rood in her hands, and choristers chanting psalms. Turgot recorded from the priest with her (he was not present) that she kissed the relic, and sang the whole of a psalm. She was reported to have given thanks to God for the agony she suffered at the end, so that she was cleansed of sins. Her body is said to have become very cold, and she then lay as if she was in agony. She died soon afterwards. It was 16 November, and this became her feast day.

She and Malcolm were eventually to be buried in Dunfermline Abbey, although he was not interred there for some 20 years after Margaret's death. Following his slaying in Northumberland, Malcolm's body was taken to Tynemouth by two local men for burial, and his remains were not returned to Scotland until the reign of Alexander I.

St Margaret's Chapel, Edinburgh Castle –
Margaret, who was very unwell, may have prayed
here before learning of the death of her husband.

When it was known that Margaret and Malcolm
were dead, Edinburgh Castle was besieged by
Malcolm's younger brother Donald Bane. Margaret's
body had to be smuggled out of the fortress by Edgar
using a path to the west of the castle, by what is now
St Cuthbert's Church. A mist descended to hide the
escape, and this has been attributed to divine
intervention. From here, she was taken to their church
of The Trinity in Dunfermline, and there laid to rest.

Margaret's life was recorded by her devoted

confessor and biographer Turgot in the *Life of Queen Margaret.* It was compiled about 1107, although it may have been added to and embellished after his death: there is no original extant copy, although there is a damaged one in the British Library. Turgot had a great affection or even love for his charge, and his biography is full of only praise (which is even less surprising bearing in mind it was commissioned by Matilda (Edith), queen of England and Margaret's daughter). Matilda united the Saxon and Norman lines to the English throne, and the account makes much of Margaret's relationship to Edward the Confessor and Edmund Ironside.

Indeed, Malcolm seems little more than a barbaric foil to his queen's devotion, piety and sophistication, an ignorant and childish thug to be redeemed by Margaret's goodness. Whether Malcolm would have recognised this portrait of himself is a moot point. Certainly his redemption did not stretch to his repeated plundering of Northumberland, although it may have financed the improvements to his court and his wife's generosity to the poor.

Turgot was prior of Durham in England, then later Bishop of St Andrews. He was deprived of this latter post by Edgar, son of Margaret, because Turgot would not repudiate his obedience (and therefore that of the church) to York and the superiority of the English church.

Margaret was canonised by the Pope in 1250 (although she was regarded as a saint by the people in Scotland from shortly after her death), the only 'Scottish' saint now recognised and venerated universally by the Roman Catholic church: there is a

statue of her at Lourdes in France as well as another
at the Scots College in Rome. Unusually Margaret
was neither martyred nor had had a particularly
difficult life, despite some people's opinion of her
husband and his rough ways – and her own relatively
austere life (austere, that is, for a queen). Margaret
was to live into her late forties, certainly a good age
for a woman of the 11th century who had had so
many children, and she had enough worldly
experience to have had eight successful births. This
perhaps explains why her popularity remains, even in
modern times: she was a married woman with
children. Most female saints of the time, as well as
being royal, had to be virgins or widows, and it says
much for her that she was canonised.

David I, her son, remodelled the church at
Dunfermline to enshrine her grave, and around 1150
had his mother's bones placed into a stone tomb
directly above her original grave. This was at the east
of the new nave of the abbey church, in front of the
rood screen which would have divided the ordinary
folk of the congregation from the monks. This meant
that the ordinary people still had access to her shrine,
which was already associated with many miracles, and
lights and sparks were said to have been seen often at
her tomb. Her fame was further increased when
William the Lyon (her great grandson) asserted he
had had a vision of her while praying at her tomb in
1199, advising him not to invade England (it would
have been opportune had he prayed to her in 1174
when William invaded England and as a result was
captured and imprisoned). Her shrine was visited by

many pilgrims, including those en route to St Andrews, and Dunfermline became one of the foremost pilgrimage sites in Scotland. In 1263, before the Battle of Largs and victory against the Vikings, a vision of Margaret is said to have been seen on a horse leaving Dunfermline Abbey for the west to help the Scottish army.

Her case for canonisation had been put strongly by the then abbot of Dunfermline. It has been suggested that his motives were somewhat more practical than might have been expected from a man of God: the upkeep of the buildings was costing the abbey dear and Margaret's elevation would increase income from pilgrims. A list of miracles attributed to her relics, however, dating from the 12th and 13th century, has been discovered in Madrid. The east end of the abbey church was remodelled with the addition of a chapel

Dunfermline Abbey Church (east end) – the plinth and some ruined walls are all that remain of Margaret's relic chapel.

for her relics.

Her remains were translated from her tomb into a bejewelled casket to be taken to her new chapel. There was a sweet smell when the tomb was opened, believed to have been the smell of sanctity and further evidence of her saintliness, but possibly as the result of the original embalming of her body. Her feast day was now to be celebrated on 19 June, the date of the translation of her relics.

The casket was carried to the high altar of the church, but could not be taken to her new chapel beyond the tomb of Malcolm. His bones were also put into the casket, and were then placed in her relic chapel at the east end of the choir. The remains of this chapel, with the pedestal on which the casket was placed, can be seen outside the present walls of the later abbey church. It seems a shame that when the new church was built in the 19th century this should have been left ruinous and open to the elements.

There are few old dedications of churches and parishes to Margaret in Scotland, probably because most parish churches had already been dedicated to older Scottish and Irish saints, such as Ninian, Palladius, Columba and Maelrubha, while others were dedicated to 'more important' saints such as Michael or the Apostles. There were dedications to Margaret at Urquhart in Moray (although only the burial ground survives, while no trace remains of the old parish church); Forgue in Aberdeenshire (again nothing remains of the old church); and Abercrombie in Fife (the ruins remain in the grounds of Balcaskie House). There may have also been dedications on Orkney: at South

St Margaret's Chapel, Edinburgh Castle – believed to date from the 12th century, but it is possible that Margaret worshipped here.

Ronaldsay near St Margaret's Hope, and on Stronsay at Clestrain.

The most famous dedication is the small chapel among the many buildings which cluster around the rocky Edinburgh Castle. Margaret and Malcolm had a residence here, probably on the highest part of the castle rock, but nothing certain remains from this period. The chapel is rectangular in plan with a semi-circular apse, and a fine arch carved with dog-toothed patterns. It is likely it was built, or remodelled anyway, after Margaret's death by her son David, although it is possible she prayed here.

Several wells were dedicated to Margaret, including below the Castle Rock at Edinburgh Castle in a now

St Margaret's Well, Holyrood Park – the well was originally at Meadowbank and the building was moved here in the 19th century.

ruined building, in Dunfermline (the site now a private garden), at Dalzell House in Lanarkshire (covered by a 19th-century building), and at Meadowbank in Edinburgh. This last well was later covered by a remarkable stone vault. The area became used for railway workshops in the 19th century, and the well building was moved to Holyrood Park. The water now appears to come from St Anthony's Well (famed for improving looks by washing the face on 1 May) further up the hill, where there is a boulder and stone basin. St Margaret's Loch, also in the park and home to many swans and ducks, also commemorates her.

There were also wells at Hound Point, near Dalmeny; at Braehead a mile or so south-west of Kelty in Fife; near the site of Raeberry Castle south of Kirkcudbright; at Hillhead of Lethenty, north of Inverurie; and at Pluscarden Abbey in Moray. These latter three were dedicated to a St Margaret, although it is possible this may have been Margaret of Antioch.

Other monarchs of Scots were also buried at Dunfermline (instead of at Iona, where Duncan and Macbeth are said to have been interred), and it became a great abbey and palace. Others mentioned in this book who were buried at Dunfermline include Margaret's sons Edward, Edmund, Ethelred, Edgar, Alexander I and David I, as well as Duncan II, Malcolm IV, Alexander III, and Robert the Bruce.

At the Reformation, from the middle of the 16th century in Scotland, pilgrimages were banned and shrines were looted and destroyed. Dunfermline Abbey was purged of idolatrous images, altars, statues and effigies, and then sacked in 1560. The abbey was then put in the charge of a commendator, administrators, not always churchmen, who enjoyed the financial benefits of the abbey's property without always undertaking the religious responsibilities. Abbot House, near the abbey and dating from 1450, was used by these commendators, and now houses a fine museum. The lands of the abbey passed to secular owners, and the buildings of the abbey deteriorated.

Mary of Guise (mother of Mary, Queen of Scots), had the remains of Margaret and Malcolm sent to Escurial, near Madrid in Spain, for safety: Philip II of Spain collected many saints' relics. A chapel, dedicated to the couple, was built there, but no longer exists.

Margaret's skull, in a bejewelled case, was removed from Dunfermline by Abbot Durie to his castle at Craigluscar, and then was taken to Edinburgh on the orders of Mary, Queen of Scots, when pregnant with James (later VI and I) in 1566. Fearing it would be despoiled, it was also taken abroad by way of Antwerp in 1597, where it was authenticated, and then to the Scots Jesuit College at Douai in northern France. The silver case, described in 1696, was encrusted with pearls and precious stones. Her auburn or fair hair was displayed in a globe of crystal. Her head was

Recreated head shrine of St Margaret (from Abbot House, Dunfermline) – the original was last seen in France in the 18th century.

seen in 1785, but may have been hidden during the French Revolution and is now assumed to be lost – although it too may now be at Escurial.

Margaret's feast day was eventually moved back to 16 November the day of her death (although not until the early 20th century), and she was made a patron saint of Scotland in 1673. Her feast day of the translation in medieval times was 19 June, although this was moved to 10 June in 1693 (the date now celebrated in the Roman Catholic Church). In art, Margaret is often represented carrying her Black Rood, and is pictured doing charitable works among the sick and poverty stricken. If anything, her popularity has grown again since the Reformation, and there are now some 20 Catholic and 10 Protestant churches dedicated to her in Scotland, and others on the Continent and in North America.

Malcolm may have had his faults, but the Scotland of his time had remained mostly united under his rule, no mean feat with such a turbulent kingdom. He lived through great upheaval, having to win his own throne back from the strong and able Macbeth and then deal with a powerful new force in Britain, the Normans. It was by his force of personality, and the support of his wife, that Scotland was bound together, a unity that was to fracture, albeit briefly, as soon as he was dead.

Margaret has been accused of playing a major part in the chaos that followed her husband's death. It is claimed that some Scots, including Malcolm's younger brother Donald Bane, may have viewed her emphasis on English or European customs and practice as a threat to their own culture. It seems far more likely, however, that ambitious men simply seized the opportunity afforded by the deaths of Margaret and Malcolm to grapple for power. Besides which, succession through the first born was not firmly established in Scotland, and Donald Bane had as good a claim to the throne as Malcolm's sons. A better claim, of course, when backed up by an army.

Whatever the truth of it, Malcolm had ruled for some 35 years, most of these with Margaret, and was probably in his sixties when he died. His marriage to Margaret was long for the time, politically expedient and apparently happy, and he left able sons to continue his dynasty. Malcolm, despite his raids into the north of England, largely avoided damaging wars with the Vikings and the Normans. The Scottish church had been revitalised, the economy was stronger, and Scotland had prospered under his long rule.

That many other kings or queens of Scots could say so much of their reigns as Margaret and Malcolm.

Scotland, however, was plunged into dynastic turmoil at their deaths, and Edgar and their other sons had to flee from Scotland and seek refuge in England.

Donald III, Donald Bane – Bane meaning 'fair' – Malcolm Canmore's brother, seized the throne, although he was not to enjoy his elevated position for long. Donald was overthrown in turn in 1094 by Duncan II – Malcolm Canmore's eldest son by Ingioborg – with English help. Duncan, however, was not popular and was soon dead: an occupational hazard for kings called Duncan.

Donald recovered the throne, this time aided by Edmund, one of the sons of Malcolm and Margaret. Edgar, Edmund's younger brother, defeated Donald and Edmund, again with an English army. Donald was blinded and imprisoned on Iona, while the disgraced Edmund retired to a monastery in England.

This was to prove only a small period of chaos, and Margaret's sons were about to assert themselves.

Sons and Descendants

Scotland was to be ruled by three of Margaret and Malcolm's sons in succession: Edgar never married and Alexander had no children so they were succeeded by their brother David. All three were pious men and shrewd kings, truly the sons of St Margaret and Malcolm Canmore.

This was to prove to be an age of relative peace, which lasted for nearly 200 years until the end of the 13th century. Edgar, who indeed was known as the Peaceable, ruled Scotland well, although he had to

Holyrood Abbey – founded by David I, who donated Margaret's Black Rood to the abbey.

give the Western Isles, including Iona, to the Norwegians to prevent war. William Rufus had died in August 1100: he was replaced by his brother Henry I, who married Matilda or Maud, also known as Edith. Edith was Margaret and Malcolm's daughter, and the marriage united the Saxon and Norman lines.

When Edgar died in 1107, he was buried beside his parents at Dunfermline Abbey. He too had endowed Dunfermline and St Andrews.

Alexander succeeded Edgar. Alexander earned his nickname The Fierce by savagely putting down a rising in Moray. However, he encouraged monastic settlements in Scotland, and founded Inchcolm Abbey, after being washed up there following a shipwreck. He married Sibylla, an illegitimate daughter of Henry I of England. This match does not appear to have been happy, and Alexander died at Stirling in 1124 without a (legitimate) son or daughter. He, too, was buried at Dunfermline, along with his wife, although whether they were united in death is not recorded.

David I followed him to the throne in 1124. He married Matilda, an English heiress, and David acquired the Earldom of Huntingdon in the Midlands of England, as well as other lands, which added much to the wealth of the country. Many new burghs, with special trading privileges, were introduced.

He reorganised the Scottish church, establishing and strengthening bishoprics and parishes, and he founded many abbeys and monastic houses, including those at Dryburgh, Holyrood in Edinburgh, Jedburgh, Kelso and Melrose. David is usually credited with the building of St Margaret's Chapel at Edinburgh Castle, although it is possible that parts of the building are older.

David had spent many years in exile in England, and during this time had become friendly with many Norman families. He invited some of these men – Bruces, Balliols, Comyns, and FitzAllans (the FitzAllans later became known as the Stewarts: they were to become the High Stewards) – to Scotland, and gave them land or married them to heiresses.

David had to put down two rebellions in his own realm, and became involved in the struggle for the English crown between Stephen of Blois and David's niece, the rightful heir, Maud or Matilda. David supported Maud and invaded England, but at the Battle of the Standard in 1138, near Northallerton in North Yorkshire, his army was crushed. Despite this loss and Stephen's eventual victory, David benefited from the confusion and acquired the Earldom of Northumberland and lands in Cumbria from the English. The kingdom of Scots reached its furthest extent southwards: Malcolm Canmore would have been proud. David died in 1153 at his prayers at Carlisle Castle. He had been one of the most successful kings of Scots, and had demonstrated how a strong Scottish monarch could use weakness and disarray in England to his benefit.

Unfortunately, his able son Henry had predeceased him, and the kingdom passed to Henry's son, the 11-year-old Malcolm IV, known as the Maiden, because he took a vow of celibacy and never married. The Earldom of Northumberland was lost, although it was not without benefit: it was exchanged for the wealthy Earldom of Huntingdon with Henry II of

England (who had come to the throne in 1154). Malcolm died at the age of 23 without any children.

William the Lyon, brother of Malcolm, became King of Scots in 1174. He was to marry Ermengarde de Beaumont, and they had a son, Alexander (later Alexander II), as well as three daughters. William tried to recover the Earldom of Northumberland in 1175 and invaded the north of England. He was captured at Alnwick, and held at Falaise in Normandy until he swore fealty to Henry II of England as his overlord, who then released him. William then devoted his energies to Scotland and brought the north of Scotland under his control and managed to get the Pope to recognise the Scottish church as being separate from that of England. William restored Scotland's independence in 1189 by promising to pay Richard the Lionheart, the then King of England who had just come to the throne, 10,000 merks.

In 1176 William had had the abbey at Arbroath built, in memory of his friend, Thomas a Becket, and when William died in 1214 he was buried there.

Alexander II was 17 years old when his father died, and was known as a lawmaker. A collection of laws, called *Regiam Majestatem*, was compiled at this time. He married Joan, daughter of John I, King of England, and then on Joan's death, Marie de Coucy, by whom he had a son, the future Alexander III.

Alexander II pursued the policy of trying to acquire Northumberland during the troubled reign of John I (1199-1216), King of England, a policy which was working until thwarted by the accession of the Henry III in 1216. Alexander II gave up any claims, although he retained the Earldom of Huntingdon and other lands in England. He switched his attention to the north and west, consolidated his hold on outlying areas, and tried to recover the Western Isles from Norway. While on an expedition in 1249 he died on Kerrera, an island near Oban. Alexander had a par-

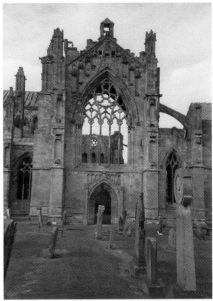

Melrose Abbey – Alexander II was buried here after dying on Kerrera.

ticular affection for Melrose Abbey, and he was buried there.

Alexander III, then only eight, came to the throne, and was married to Margaret, the 11-year-old daughter of Henry III, King of England, in 1251. This is often seen as a golden age in Scotland. Alexander managed to keep peace with England but also managed to maintain independence, and the nation prospered during his long reign as he further strengthened royal authority.

His attention was focused on the north. He ravaged the island of Skye in an attempt to wrest the Western Isles from Norway. A fleet of Norse long ships was launched against the Scots, but was wrecked by a storm, and a reduced force of Norwegians was defeated at the Battle of Largs in 1263. Three years later the Treaty of Perth confirmed that the Western Isles and the Isle of Man were ceded to the Scots. St Margaret is said to have appeared to Scottish troops before the battle, and a cairn at Largs was known as Margaret's Law.

Margaret, Alexander's wife, died in 1275 at the age of only 35, and their elder son, also called Alexander, died in 1284. Alexander III had no other surviving children, no close heir to take the throne on his death. In 1285 he was wed to the young and beautiful Yolande de Dreux. But it was not to be. On a stormy night Alexander decided to see his wife in Fife. The crossing at Queensferry was perilous, yet he made it safely. But it was a black night, and he lost his way in the dark and fell to his death off cliffs at Kinghorn. The year was 1286.

> When Alexander our king wis deid
> That Scotland led in lauche and le[1]
> Away was sonse[2] of ale and breid
> Of wine and wax[3], of gamin and glee
> Our gold was changit into leid
> The fruit failet on every tree
> Christ succour Scotland and remeid
> That stade[4] us in perplexitie
>
> Anonymous

---

[1] law and peace   [2] plenty   [3] wassail cake   [4] beset

What Happened Afterwards

Apart from the brief, although bitter, turmoil following Margaret and Malcolm's deaths, Scotland had done well under the rule of their sons and descendants. Although fighting did break out, both with England, with Norway, and with factions from within Scotland, this was a period of relative peace, consolidation and prosperity. The kings strengthened their power in areas such as Galloway and Moray, and after the Battle of Largs in 1263 Scotland gained the Western Isles. During this time, much of the Gaelic influence, at least in lowland areas, diminished, and Scotland became a small but strong and relatively united kingdom within Europe.

Not one of the kings that reigned from Edgar to Alexander was to die in battle or to be murdered by his subjects: quite a feat compared to the kings who had come before and those that were to follow. The latter part of this period has been called the Golden Age of Scotland, although this may be as much in comparison as to what was follow and the devastation inflicted on Scotland by the aggression of the English.

With the death of Alexander III (Alexander was also buried at Dunfermline Abbey), and the end of the direct Canmore line, Scotland was to be plunged into dynastic strife, warfare and invasion by the English that would threaten the very existence of the Kingdom of Scots. For several months it was hoped that Yolande de Dreux was pregnant, and would produce an heir: but these hopes proved fruitless. The next direct descendant was Margaret, the Maid of Norway, granddaughter of Alexander III (Alexander's daughter, also Margaret, had married the King of Norway, but she died before her father). The Maid of Norway, no more than a child, was summoned to Scotland four years later, but she died in Orkney on the journey south.

There were now no close heirs but there were numerous competitors who had a claim to the Scottish throne, mostly through the daughters of David, Earl of Huntingdon (grandson of David I and the brother of Malcolm the Maiden and William the Lyon). The main competitors were two great magnates of Scotland: Robert the Bruce, grandfather of Robert I the Bruce, and John Balliol, later John I.

Fearing civil war and chaos, the Scots asked Edward I of England, who had come to the throne in 1272 and had previously been friendly with the Scots, to mediate in the dispute between the competitors. This he did, choosing John Balliol to be king, but first making him swear allegiance to Edward as his overlord. Balliol struggled to assert himself against Edward, but in 1296 Edward I and the English invaded, slaughtering the inhabitants of Berwick and routing the Scottish army at Dunbar. So began the Scottish Wars of Independence, a struggle which was to continue in one form or another for hundreds of years.

The legacy of Margaret and Malcolm was the foundation of a strong and united nation, which would be tested to the full but would resist the aggression of England. Scotland would remain a small but independent kingdom through 500 years of invasion and fighting, until a future King of Scots, James VI, united the thrones of the two countries.

Statue of St Margaret at St Margaret's Cave, beneath Chalmers Street Car Park, in Dunfermline.

Map 2: Places of Interest

The notes below refer to the entries on the following pages:
Properties managed by Historic Scotland are indicated by (HS) contact:
0131 668 8800 email: hs.explorer@scotland.gsi.gov.uk
National Trust for Scotland properties are indicated by (NTS).
Opening time are inclusive unless otherwise stated. Most manned
sites are closed at Christmas and New Year: tel to confirm.
Admission prices: £ up to £2.50; ££ between £2.50 and £5.00;
£££ more than £5.00. To confirm opening, or if there is any doubt
about access to sites, please check with the sites, check locally with
tourist information centres, or check with land owners.

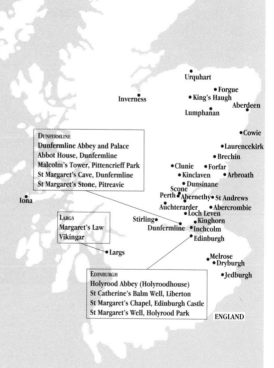

Places of Interest

Below is a list of some of the places associated with St Margaret and
Malcolm Canmore. The most impressive and interesting are centred
around Dunfermline Abbey, although the small chapel at Edinburgh Castle
is also particularly fine. Sites in Dunfermline include the abbey church
itself with the base of Margaret's shrine, the scant remains of Malcolm's
Tower in the picturesque Pittencrieff Park, the atmospheric St Margaret's
Cave under the Chalmer's Street car park and reached by 87 steps down
a tunnel, and St Margaret's Stone between Rosyth and Dunfermline, as
well as displays and information about Margaret and Malcolm at Abbot
House just next to the abbey. As well as St Margaret's Chapel at Edinburgh
Castle, there is St Margaret's Well in Holyrood Park and Holyrood Abbey.
Also included are a selection of the best abbeys founded by Margaret's
sons and descendants, including Arbroath, Dryburgh, Holyrood, Inchcolm,
Jedburgh, and Melrose, information about some of the old churches
dedicated to Margaret, and palaces or strongholds held by Malcolm.

Abbot House, Dunfermline

*Off A994, just north of Dunfermline Abbey, in Maygate, Dunfermline,
Fife (NGR: NT 089875 LR: 65)*

The heritage centre has fas-
cinating displays on St Margaret, Malcolm Canmore
and the nearby abbey, as
well as the recreated head
shrine of St Margaret. It cov-
ers the story of Scotland
from Pictish to modern
times, including William
Wallace, Robert the Bruce,
Robert Henryson, Charles I,
and Andrew Carnegie. The
building dates from the 15th
century, and was built for
the abbots of Dunfermline
Abbey. Occupiers have in-

cluded Anne of Denmark, the wife of James VI; and Lady Anne Halkett, Jacobite, herbalist and midwife.

Guides. Explanatory displays. Video. Gift shop. Restaurant with outside seating in garden (overlooking abbey). Scented garden. WC. Disabled access to ground floor and WC. Disabled parking only; public car parks within 600 yards. Group concessions (pre-booked). £ (Upstairs exhib only).

Open all year, daily 10.00-17.00, last admission to upper floors Mar-Oct 16.15, Nov-Feb 15.15; closed Christmas Day and New Year's Day. Tel: 01383 733266 Fax: 01383 624908 Web: www.abbothouse.co.uk Email: dht@abbothouse.fsnet.co.uk

Abercrombie Church

Off B942, 1 mile north of St Monans, E of Abercrombie, W of Balcaskie House, Fife. (NGR: NO 522035 LR: 59)

The ruinous remains of the church of the former parish of Abercrombie. It was rectangular in plan and had corbiestepped gables, and was dedicated to St Margaret. It was granted to Dunfermline Abbey in 1165, has some sculpted stones built into the fabric, and stands in an old burial ground. The Abercrombies of nearby Balcaskie were buried here.

In the grounds of Balcaskie House.

Aberdeen

Off A956, centre of Aberdeen. (NGR: NJ 942060? LR: 38)

There is said to have been a royal palace in Aberdeen, a property of Malcolm Canmore in the 11th century, and given to the Trinitarian friary. There are apparently some medieval remains at the site.

Abernethy (HS)

On A913, 6 miles SE of Perth, Perthshire. (NGR: NO 190165 LR: 58)

Malcolm Canmore met William the Conqueror here. Malcolm had to come to terms in 1072 after the Normans had invaded, and Malcolm 'agreed to be William's man', although it is not clear what this meant. There was also a Culdee community here, and the imposing round tower, probably dating from the 11th century, is all that remains of an important and ancient monastic centre. There are fine views from the top, and a Pictish carved stone at the base. A museum is located at School Wynd in Abernethy.

Parking Nearby

Open Apr-Sep – for access apply to key holder.

Tel: 0131 668 8800 (tower)/01738 850889 (museum)

Alexander III Monument, Kinghorn

On A921, 3 miles S of Kirkcaldy, E of Kinghorn, Fife.
(NGR: NT 254864   LR: 66)

The monument, standing on King's Crag, marks where Alexander III fell from his horse over cliffs and was killed on the night of 18 March 1286. Alexander was on his way to Kinghorn to see his new bride, and his death threw Scotland into dynastic troubles which culminated in the Wars of Independence against the English.

Car parking.

Access at all reasonable times.

Arbroath Abbey (HS)

Off A92, Arbroath, Angus. (NGR: NO 643413   LR: 54)

The substantial and picturesque ruins remain of a Tironsenian abbey, founded in 1178 by William the Lyon (who was buried here in 1214), in

memory of his friend Thomas a Becket. Part of the church survives, including the fine west end, the gatehouse, sacristy and Abbot's House, which houses a museum. The cloister and other domestic buildings are very ruinous. The famous Declaration of Arbroath was signed here in 1320, about which there us an exhibition. The Stone of Destiny was found at Arbroath after being taken from Westminster Abbey in 1951 – the Stone is now at Edinburgh Castle.

Explanatory displays in visitor centre and Abbot's House. Audio-visual presentations. Gift shop. WC (disabled). Wheelchair access. Parking. £.

Open all year: Apr-Sep, daily 9.30-18.30; Oct-Mar, Mon-Sat 9.00-16.30, closed Thu PM and Fri, Sun 14.00-16.30.

Tel: 01241 878756

Auchterarder

Off A824, 0.5 miles N of Auchterarder, Castleton, Perthshire.
(NGR: NN 936133 LR: 58)

Malcolm Canmore is said to have had a hunting seat here, but the first written reference is in 1277. Edward I of England stayed at the castle in 1296. Little remains except some walls with gunloops and earthworks, probably dating from much later than the 11th century.

Brechin Cathedral

Off A90, Brechin, Angus. (NGR: NO 596601 LR: 44)

The fine atmospheric building, which was dedicated to The Holy Trinity, is still used as a parish church, and dates from the 13th century. Adjacent

is an unusual 11th-century round tower, probably from a Culdee community and usually thought to be modelled on Irish counterparts, and believed to have been used to store precious relics. Only two of these towers survive in Scotland, the other being at Abernethy. There is a fine Pictish cross-slab, and other fragments, including the 9th-century St Mary's Stone, and there are some interesting markers in the burial ground.

Parking nearby. Sales area.
Cathedral: open all year, daily 9.00-17.00.
Tel: 01356 629360

Clunie Castle

Off A923, 4.5 miles W of Blairgowrie, N of Clunie, W of Loch of Clunie, Perthshire. (NGR: NO 111440 LR: 53)

Not much remains of Clunie Castle, said to have been the site of a palace of Malcolm Canmore. It was a royal castle, and Edward I of England stayed here in 1296. It had been completely demolished by the beginning of the 16th century and materials were used to build the nearby tower house [NO 114440].

Cowie Castle

Off A92, 1.5 miles NE of Stonehaven, near St Mary's ruined church, Aberdeenshire. (NGR: NO 887874   LR: 45)

The castle was traditionally built by Malcolm Canmore, and Cowie was apparently made a burgh in the 11th century. There are traces of a stone wall cutting off the coastal promontory. The castle was probably dismantled early in the 14th century. The property was held by the Frasers, and Alexander Fraser of Cowie was Chamberlain to Robert the Bruce. He was slain at the Battle of Dupplin Moor in 1329.

Dryburgh Abbey (HS)

Off B6356 or B6404, 8 miles SE of Melrose, Dryburgh, Borders.
(NGR: NT 591317   LR: 73)

A picturesque and substantial ruin in a fine setting by the River Tweed, the abbey was founded by David I as a Premonstratensian establishment, dedicated to St Mary. Most of the buildings date from the 12th and 13th centuries, and part of the church survives, as do substantial portions of the cloister, including the fine chapter house, parlour and vestry. The Abbey was burnt by the English in 1322, 1385, and 1544. Sir Walter Scott is buried here.

Gift shop. WC. Picnic area. Disabled access. Car and coach parking. WC. Group concessions. £.

Open all year: Apr-Sep, daily 9.30-18.30; Oct-Mar, Mon-Sat 9.30-16.30, Sun 14.00-16.30.

Tel: 01835 822381

Dunfermline Abbey and Palace (HS)

Off A994, Monastery Street, Dunfermline, Fife. (NGR: NT 089872   LR: 65)

Malcolm and Margaret founded or extended a church here sometime after 1070, the site occupied by the nave of the abbey church (the foundations are marked out on the floor) and they may have been married here. This was an older Christian site, and Dunfermline was an important Pictish centre. The abbey (or a priory) was probably founded by Margaret as a

small Benedictine house, although it was not until the reign of David I that the large abbey church was built. Margaret and Malcolm were buried here, Margaret before the rood screen so that ordinary folk could visit her shrine. Dunfermline became a major centre of pilgrimage, and the choir was extended in the 13th century with the addition of a new relic chapel for her shrine at the east end, as well as aisles (walled off from the choir), so that pilgrims could visit her chapel without disturbing the monks!

The abbey was sacked in 1560 after the Reformation, and the choir was demolished. A new cruciform parish church, with a central tower, bearing the legend King Robert the Bruce, was built on the site in the 19th century. The ruin of Margaret's relic chapel was not incorporated into this new building, and survives outside the east end of this church with the plinth on which her shrine rested. The new parish church has a fine carved pulpit and lectern, stained glass and funerary monuments.

The nave (or 'Old Church') with its two towers (one modern after the original collapsed in 1807), survives from the 12th-century church, and resembles Durham Cathedral. It was used as the parish church after the Reformation, and was altered for Protestant worship. The church, both old and new, is surrounded by an interesting burial ground with fine views.

Other Scottish monarchs of this time were buried at Dunfermline, including Duncan II, Edgar, Alexander I, David I, Malcolm IV, Alexander III (apart from his heart, which is interred at St John's Kirk in Perth), and Robert the Bruce (apart from his heart, which is buried at Melrose). Bruce's grave was rediscovered in the 19th century, and is marked by a large brass

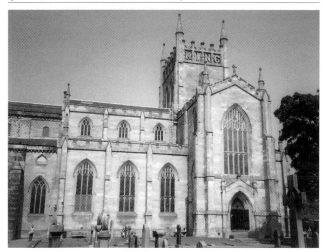

panel on the floor. A plaster cast of his skull is also on display.

Abbot George Durie, the last abbot, was responsible for removing the relics of Margaret (except her head) and Malcolm to the continent. Their relics ended up in Madrid with the King of Spain, although the Jesuits of Douai in France acquired Margaret's head. Their relics are now lost.

There appears to have been a Royal Palace at Dunfermline from the 14th century or earlier, and Edward I stayed here in 1303-4 (although also see Malcolm's Tower, which is located nearby in Pittencrieff Park). David II was born at the palace in 1323, and James I was born here in 1394. James IV, James V, and Mary, Queen of Scots, all visited. The palace was remodelled in 1587 by Queen Anne, wife of James VI, and Charles I was born here in 1600.

The church (both nave and new church), surviving domestic buildings of the abbey, and the remains of the palace are open to the public.

Explanatory displays. Gift shop (HS and in new church). Parking nearby. £.
Nave church and palace ruins (HS), open Apr-Sep, daily 9.30-18.30; Oct-Mar, Mon-Sat 9.30-16.30, Sun 14.00-16.30, closed Thu PM and Fri. Choir/New (parish) church, open Apr-end Oct, Mon-Sat 10.00-16.30, Sun 14.00-16.30; closed for wedding.
Tel: 01383 739026 (HS)   Fax: 01383 739026 (HS)
Web: www.dunfabbey.freeserve.co.uk (parish church)
Email: tourism@dunfabbey.freeserve.co.uk (parish church)

Dunsinane Hill

Off B953, 7 miles NE of Perth, Dunsinane, Perthshire. (NGR: NO 214316 LR: 53)

The summit of Dunsinane Hill is surrounded by lines of defences, known as 'Macbeth's Castle', and this is traditionally where Macbeth awaited the forces of Earl Siward and Malcolm Canmore – and most of Birnam Wood (which although some 12 miles away, can be seen from the summit). According to the play, Macbeth was killed at the battle – but although it is likely Macbeth was defeated here (or possibly at Scone) in 1054, it was not until 1057 that he was slain, and that was at Lumphanan.

The hill is reached by a steep footpath on the N side of the hill.

Edinburgh Castle (HS)

Off A1, in the centre of Edinburgh. (NGR: NT 252735 LR: 66)

Standing on a high rock, Edinburgh Castle was one of the strongest and most important fortresses in Scotland. It was occupied from prehistoric times, and Malcolm Canmore had a fortress here, at which Margaret died

in 1093 on hearing of the slaying of her husband. The oldest building is the small Norman chapel of the early 12th century, dedicated to St Margaret, with a semi-circular apse. The inside of the chapel is whitewashed, and the decorated chancel arch survives. A copy of St Margaret's gospel book can be seen here, and there are fine stained-glass windows.

The castle had an English garrison from 1296 until 1313 during the Wars of Independence, when the Scots, led by Thomas Randolph, climbed the rock, surprised the garrison, and retook it. The castle was slighted, but there was an English garrison here again until 1341, when it was retaken by a Scots' force disguised as merchants. In 1367-71 David II rebuilt the castle with strong curtain walls and towers, and a large L-plan keep, David's Tower, which was named after him.

After the murder of the young Earl of Douglas and his brother at the 'Black Dinner' at the castle in 1440, it was attacked and captured by the Douglases after a nine-month siege, and required substantial repairs. In 1566 Mary, Queen of Scots, gave birth to the future James VI in the castle, after having removed the head shrine of St Margaret from Dunfermline Abbey when pregnant in 1566. The shrine was taken to Antwerp, and was then acquired by the Jesuits of Douai in northern France. The shrine was lost during the French Revolution. After Mary's abdication, the castle was held on her behalf, until English help forced it to surrender in 1573. The well, below the castle in Princes Street Gardens with a ruined building, was known as St Margaret's Well, and used by the garrison.

The castle was captured in 1640 after a three-month siege by the Covenanters, and Cromwell besieged it throughout the autumn of 1650. The Jacobites failed to take it in both the 1715 and 1745 Risings, and many of the present buildings date from the 17th and 18th centuries.

The castle is the home of the Scottish crown jewels, and the Stone of Destiny (or Stone of Scone) – on which the Kings of Scots were inaugurated, including Malcolm Canmore (at Scone) and his successors – and is an interesting complex of buildings, not least the Great Hall and Half Moon Battery, with spectacular views over the capital. Other features include the Scottish War Memorial, the Regimental Museum of the Royal Scots, and Mons Meg, a massive 15th-century cannon.

Explanatory displays. Audio-guide tour. Guided tours. Gift and book shops. Cafe. WC. Disabled access. Visitors with a disability can be taken to the top of the castle by a courtesy vehicle; ramps and lift access to Crown Jewels and Stone of Destiny. Car and coach parking (except during Tattoo). £££+.

Open all year: Apr-Sep, daily 9.30-17.15 (last ticket sold); Oct-Mar, daily 9.30-16.15 (last ticket sold), castle closes 45 mins after last ticket sold; times may be altered during Tattoo and state occasions; closed 25/26 Dec.

Tel: 0131 225 9846

Forfar Castle

To W of Forfar, near A926 north of junction with A929, east of Loch of Forfar. (NGR: NO 456507 LR: 54)

The castle, nothing of which survives, was associated with Malcolm Canmore and Margaret, and St Margaret's Inch, now a promontory since the loch was drained, is located in the loch. There was said to be a chapel here, dedicated to The Holy Trinity, and a cell of Coupar Angus Abbey is recorded in 1234. The castle was used by William the Lyon and Alexander II. It was garrisoned by the English during the Wars of Independence, and was visited by Edward I in 1296, but was recaptured by the Scots, who slaughtered the garrison on Christmas day 1308, then demolished the defences. It was apparently rebuilt, then captured and slighted again in 1313. It had been abandoned by the 1330s. The Meffan in Forfar is a fine museum, and has good displays on Forfar and the Picts.

Site accessible at all reasonable times.

Forgue Old Parish Church

On B9091, 6 miles NE of Huntly, Forgue, Aberdeenshire. (NGR: NJ 611451 LR: 29)

Nothing remains of the old parish church, which was dedicated to St Margaret, and stood on a knoll. It lay just to the south of the present large building of 1858, itself replacing a church of 1795. There are remains of a 17th-century pew in this church – the building could hold 900 people. In the burial ground are some interesting memorials, including a burial aisle for the Morrisons of Bognie.

Access to burial ground at all reasonable times.

Holyrood Abbey, Edinburgh (HS)

Edinburgh, foot of the Royal Mile, adjacent to Holyrood Palace. (NGR: NT 269740 LR: 66)

The fine ruined nave of the church of the Augustinian abbey, founded by David I in 1128, survives beside the Palace of Holyroodhouse.

David presented the Black Rood of Scotland, which had been held by Margaret when she died, to the abbey, and hence the name of the abbey ('rood' or 'rude' means cross). The Black Rood was stolen by the English during the Wars of Independence, and, although returned to Scotland, was lost at the Battle of Neville's Cross in 1346 and then kept at Durham

Cathedral in England. It was lost at the Reformation. An alternative version of the founding of the abbey is that David was attacked by a stag in the nearby hunting park and was saved when a vision of the cross appeared between the stag's antlers.

The English sacked the abbey in 1322 and 1385, doing much damage. David II (son of Robert the Bruce), James V and Henry Stewart, Lord Darnley, are buried in the church, although their tombs were despoiled by the English in another attack of 1544.

The nave continued to be used as the parish church after the Reformation, although the rest of the abbey was demolished and little else survives. The roof of the nave itself collapsed in 1768 and building was abandoned for worship.

Developed from the guest house of the abbey, the Palace of Holyroodhouse was remodelled by successive monarchs into a magnificent courtyard palace, and it remains the official residence of the monarch in Scotland.

St Margaret's Well is located near the palace in Holyrood Park.

Holyroodhouse: guided tours: Nov-Mar. Gift shop. WC. Garden. Disabled access. Car and coach parking nearby. £££.

Open as Holyroodhouse: open all year (except when the monarch is in residence – Good Friday and 25-26 Dec): Apr-Oct, daily 9.30-17.15; Nov-Mar, daily 9.30-15.45.

Tel: 0131 556 1096/7371   Fax: 0131 557 5256

Web: www.royal-collection.gov.uk

Email: holyrood@royalcollection.org.uk

Inchcolm Abbey (HS)

Inchcolm, 6.5 miles SE of Kirkcaldy, island in the Firth of Forth, Fife. (NGR: NT 191827 LR: 66)

The abbey was dedicated to St Columba, and founded in 1123 by Alexander I after he had been rescued here from the sea, his boat having capsized crossing the Forth at Queensferry. He was washed up on Inchcolm and given refuge by a hermit. The abbey was sacked by the English in 1542 and 1547, and garrisoned by the French in 1548.

 Although ruined, this is the best preserved monastic complex in Scotland, the cloister and chapter house being complete, and there is a small cell, said to have been used by the hermit who helped Alexander.

   The island was later used as a naval quarantine station, fort, and Russian naval hospital, and had gun emplacements built to defend the Forth Bridge during World War II. The island is also known for seals and wildlife.

Exhibition. Explanatory boards. Gift shop. Picnic area. WC. Disabled access. £ + ferry.

Open Apr-Sep, daily 9.30-18.30; ferry (£) (30 mins) from South or North Queensferry (ferry into tel: 0131 331 4857)

Tel: 0131 331 4857 (HS)

Iona Abbey (HS)

Off unlisted road, Iona, Argyll. (NGR: NM 287245 LR: 48)

Situated on the beautiful and peaceful island of Iona, this is where Columba came to form a monastic community, and from where he reputedly converted the northern Picts of mainland Scotland. Columba's shrine, within the Abbey buildings, dates from the 9th century. Many of the early Kings of Scots are buried in 'Reilig Odhrain' Oran's cemetery by the 'Street of the Dead' – as well as kings of Ireland, France and Norway: 48 Scottish, 8 Norwegian and 4 Irish kings according to one 16th-century source. Among the kings buried here are said to be both Duncan and Macbeth. The 11th-century chapel of St Oran also survives, and may have been built on the orders of Margaret. The magnificent St Martin's Cross and St John's Cross stand just outside the church, and the Infirmary Museum houses one of the largest collections of early Christian carved stones in Europe.

   The abbey was abandoned after raids by the Vikings, but was re-established by Margaret and Malcolm in the 11th century, and she may have had St Oran's Chapel built. It was refounded as a Benedictine establishment in 1203 by Reginald, son of Somerled, and dedicated to the Virgin Mary. Although the buildings became ruinous after the Reformation, the abbey church was rebuilt from 1899-1910, and the cloister was restored in 1936 for the Iona Community.

Between the abbey and the nunnery is MacLean's Cross, a fine 15th-century carved stone cross. The ruinous Augustinian nunnery of St Mary was founded in 1208, and the St Columba Centre at Fionnphort on Mull features an exhibition about the Celtic church, Iona and St Columba. The centre also provides information on the local area.

Day tours from Oban in summer. Explanatory displays. Gift shop. Tearoom. WC. Picnic area. Car and coach parking at Fionnphort. £ (ferry). £ (admission).

Open all year: Apr-Sep, daily 9.30-18.30; Oct-Mar, daily 9.30-16.30; last ticket 30 mins before closing – ferry from Fionnphort (£), no cars on Iona. Walk to abbey; St Columba Centre open Apr-Sep, 11.00-17.00.

Jedburgh Abbey (HS)

On A68, Jedburgh, Borders. (NGR: NT 650204 LR: 74)

Jedburgh Abbey, which was founded by David I about 1138 as an Augustinian abbey, is now ruinous, but much of the impressive Romanesque and early Gothic church survives, as do some remains of the domestic buildings. The Abbey was sacked numerous times by the English, and after an attack in 1544-5 the ruined monastic buildings were then used as a quarry. The church was used by the parish until 1875 when the crown arch and vaulting of the crossing collapsed, and, although unroofed, is in a good

state of preservation. There is a fine rose window in the west front and richly carved Norman doorway.

The cloister and other buildings are ruinous but picturesque, and there is a fine herb garden.

Visitor centre. Exhibition. Explanatory panels. Gift shop. Tearoom. Picnic area. Limited disabled access and WC. Parking. ££.

Open all year: Apr-Sep, daily 9.30-18.30; Oct-Mar, Mon-Sat 9.30-16.30, Sun 14.00-16.30; last ticket 30 mins before closing; closed 25/26 Dec. Tel: 01835 863925

Kinclaven Castle

Off A93, 5 miles S of Blairgowrie, 0.5 miles E of Kinclaven Farm, Perthshire. (NGR: NO 158377 LR: 53)

Kinclaven Castle is a very ruined rectangular castle of enclosure, possibly dating from the 11th century, with the remains of a keep. Ditches protected the castle on the landward side, and it was a place of great strength. A castle was built here by Alexander II around 1230-40 on the site of an older stronghold, said to have been used by Malcolm Canmore in the 11th century. Edward I stayed here in 1296 and it was held by the English until 1297, when it was captured and slighted by William Wallace in 1299. It was taken by forces under Edward III in 1335, but was destroyed in 1336. The castle remained a royal castle, and would appear to still have been in use as late as 1455.

King's Haugh

Off A941, 8 miles S of Dufftown, King's Haugh, Moray. (NGR: NJ 363303 LR: 37)

Possible site of stronghold or residence of Malcolm Canmore.

Laurencekirk Parish Church

On A937 near junction with B9120, Laurencekirk, Mearns. (NGR: NO 718716 LR: 45)

Formerly known as Conventh, there was a church here from the 12th century or earlier, dedicated to St Laurence. This may have been where Margaret was prevented from visiting, apparently by divine intervention. She was on pilgrimage to a shrine of St Laurence, but apparently women were forbidden from entering it. A stone is said to have been found here, carved with a man being burnt on a grid iron, and identified as an image of St Laurence, who was martyred in the 3rd century. The present church dates from 1804, and was altered in 1819, and stands on a bank above a river. There is an old burial ground with some interesting memorials.

Loch Leven Priory (HS)

Off B996, 2.5 miles SE of Kinross, island in Loch Leven, Perth and Kinross. (NGR: NO 162003   LR: 58)

Also known as Portmoak Priory and St Serf's Priory, there was a Christian community here from early times, and the island is associated with St Serf, who probably founded a monastery here in the 8th century. It became a Culdee community, and a grant of land was confirmed to the community by Margaret and Malcolm Canmore. It became an Augustinian priory. Andrew Wyntoun, author of *The Orygynale Cronykil of Scotland*, was prior of Loch Leven from 1395.

   Little remains above ground except one rectangular building, probably 12th century, on the south-east of the island, which may have been the nave of the priory church. There are also foundations of a larger building. Excavation in 1877 uncovered the remains of two individuals, said to be St Ronan and Graham, Bishop of St Andrews.

   Lochleven Castle stands on an island in the loch, and is also in the care of Historic Scotland. Mary, Queen of Scots, was imprisoned here. It is open to the public in the summer, and reached by a ferry from Kinross. **The priory is on an island in a Nature Reserve and is not accessible to the public; castle open Apr-Sep, 9.30-17.15 (last outward ferry).**

Lumphanan

Off A93, 5 miles NE of Aboyne, Lumphanan, Kincardine & Deeside. (NGR: NJ 575034   LR: 37)

It was at Lumphanan that Macbeth was slain in 1057 by the forces of Malcolm Canmore. Macbeth's Stone [NJ 575034] is said to be where he died and Macbeth's Well [NJ 580039] where he drank before the battle. Macbeth's Cairn [NJ 578053] is where he is believed to have been buried (although it is said he was eventually interred on Iona), although it is the remains of a prehistoric burial cairn.

   Nearby are the earthworks of Peel Ring of Lumphanan – open to the public and in the care of Historic Scotland. It was held by the Durwards in the 13th century, and visited by Edward I of England in 1296.
Access at all reasonable times.

Macbeth's Castle, Inverness

Off A82, E of Inverness, The Crown. (NGR: NH 674456 LR: 26)

There is said to have been a stronghold here, the site occupied by housing. It was reputedly held by Macbeth in the 11th century, and was destroyed by Malcolm Canmore in 1057. Inverness was strategically important, and David I and William the Lyon built a keep and courtyard at another site [NH 667451]. After seeing much action, it was finally captured and blown up by the Jacobites in 1746 after the Battle of Culloden. A mock castle of 1835, housing the Sheriff Court, was built on the site, and part of the castle houses a small exhibition. There is a large statue of Flora MacDonald.

Malcolm's Tower, Dunfermline

Off A994, not far W of the Abbey, in Dunfermline [Pittencrieff] Park, Fife. (NGR: NT 087873 LR: 65)

Standing in the large and picturesque park just below the west end of the abbey, Malcolm's Tower was a large tower, of which only some of the tumbled base survives, although the remains have been landscaped. There

is said to have been a stronghold here from the 11th century, and the castle gets its name from Malcolm Canmore. It is believed that Malcolm and Margaret were married here, and it was at the tower that Edith or Maud, later wife of Henry I of England, was born. The park has many attractions, including Pittencrieff House, play parks, refreshments, fine walks and gardens.

Park: Refreshments. WC. Disabled WC. Picnic area. Parking.
Park open all year.

Margaret's Law, Largs

Off A78, to SE of Largs, Ayrshire. (NGR: NS 209586 LR: 63)

The remains of a chambered burial cairn, known as Margaret's Law and Haco's Grave. The first commemorates the association with Margaret, who is said to have appeared to Scottish troops before the Battle of Largs in

1263; the second with the defeat of the Norsemen, and supposed death of Hakon, King of Norway. In fact, Hakon survived and returned north, getting as far as Orkney, where he died in the Bishop's Palace. This was a prehistoric chambered burial cairn, although the cairn of stones has been removed and all that survives are the ruins of the chambers. Remains of several individuals were found during excavations.

Signpost at monument: Haylie Chambered Cairn.

Melrose Abbey (HS)

Off A7 or A68, in Melrose, Borders. (NGR: NT 550344   LR: 73)

An elegant and picturesque ruin, Melrose Abbey was founded as a Cistercian house by David I about 1136, and dedicated to the Blessed Virgin Mary. The church is particularly well preserved, while the domestic buildings and the cloister are very ruinous. The Abbey suffered in the wars with the English, and was sacked in 1322, 1385 and 1545. After the Reformation, the nave of the church was used as a parish church from 1618 until 1810, when it was finally abandoned. The heart of Robert the Bruce is buried in the nave, and many of the powerful Douglas family are also interred here. Alexander II had a particular affection for the abbey, and was buried here after dying on Kerrera in 1249.

Visitor centre. Audioguide available. Museum in former Commendator's House. Gift shop. Refreshments. WC. Wheelchair access. Disabled WC. Picnic area. Car and coach parking (£). ££.

Open all year, Apr-Sep 9.30-18.30, Oct-Mar, Mon-Sat 9.30-16.30, Sun 12.30-16.40; closed 25/26 Dec.

Tel: 01896 822562

Scone

Off A93, 2 miles N of Perth, Scone, Perthshire. (NGR: NO 114267   LR: 58)

The Kings of Scots were inaugurated at the Moot Hill, in the grounds of and near Scone Palace, from the reign of Kenneth MacAlpin, including Malcolm Canmore on 25 April 1057. The ceremony involved the Stone of Destiny, also called the Stone of Scone, which was kept here until thieved and taken to Westminster Abbey by Edward I of England in 1296. It was returned to Edinburgh Castle in 1996, where it is now kept with the Scottish Regalia. Malcolm may have defeated Macbeth near Scone, rather that at Dunsinane, in 1053. An abbey was founded here in the 12th century, but there are no remains after it was sacked by a Reforming mob in 1559. The last king to be inaugurated here was Charles II in 1651.

Scone Palace, a large castellated mansion dating from 1802, incorporates part of the palace built by the Ruthvens in the 1580s, itself probably created out of the Abbot's Lodging.

Scone Palace: Collections of furniture, clocks, needlework and porcelain. Gift shops. Restaurant. Tearoom. WC. Picnic area. 100 acres of wild gardens. Maze. Adventure playground. Disabled access to state rooms & restaurant. Car and coach parking. £££.

Open Apr-Oct, daily 9.30-17.15; last admission 16.45; grounds close at 17.45; other times by appt.

Tel: 01738 552300 Fax: 01738 552588

Web: www.scone-palace.co.uk   Email: visits@scone-palace.co.uk

St Andrews Cathedral (HS)

Off A91, St Andrews, Fife. (NGR: NO 516166 LR: 59)

St Regulus, or Rule, is said to have founded a monastery here in the 5th, 6th or 7th century, and may have had a relic of St Andrew. Alternatively, the relics of St Andrew were brought here in 733 by Acca, Abbot of Hexham. The Bishopric was transferred from Abernethy in 908, and there was a Culdee community at St Andrews, then known as Kilrymont.

Margaret venerated St Andrew and was concerned with helping pilgrims visit his shrine. She improved communications to St Andrews and founded a free ferry and hostels for pilgrims at Queensferry. St Rule's Church, of which the tower and part of the chancel survive, may have been built some time after 1070 for Margaret, although it may date from the first half of the 12th century. Alexander I reorganised the church and under Bishop Robert the Augustinian Order displaced the Culdee community. St Andrews became a major place of pilgrimage. St Rule's Tower is open to the public, and there are magnificent views from the top.

By the middle of the 12th century, it was decided St Rule's Church was too small, and a large new cathedral was begun nearby, the biggest in Scotland and one of the biggest in the UK, although it took many years to complete. The building was consecrated in 1318, but had to be rebuilt after a fire in 1380. After the Reformation in the middle of the 16th century, the buildings fell into disuse and many were demolished, leaving the cathedral impressive, picturesque but very ruinous. The massive precinct wall, with towers and gates, is well preserved.

The museum, housed in part of the former cloister of the priory attached to the cathedral, has a large and magnificent collection of Christian and early medieval sculpture, including cross-slabs, effigies, and other relics, as well as the St Andrews Sarcophagus. The ruins of the bishop's castle are nearby, in the care of Historic Scotland, and are open to the public.

Visitor centre and museum. Explanatory boards. Gift shop. Car parking nearby. Group concessions. £. Combined ticket for cathedral & castle is available (££).

Museum and St Rule's Tower – Open all year: Apr-Sep, daily 9.30-18.30; Oct-Mar, daily 9.30-16.30; last ticket sold 30 mins before closing; closed 25/26 Dec; cathedral ruins accessible at all reasonable times.

Tel: 01334 472563

St Catherine's Balm Well, Liberton

Off A701, 3.5 miles SE of Edinburgh Castle, Howdenhall Road, Liberton, Edinburgh. (NGR: NT 272684   LR: 66)

The well in the garden of St Catherine's, which was dedicated to Catherine of Alexandria, was believed to be a healing well for skin conditions such as eczema and possibly leprosy. The water bubbles through oil shale, and a black tarry scum floats on the surface. One story about the origin of the well is that it sprang from a drop of holy oil which was being transported from the Holy Land to Margaret, who is said to have been interested in the site. The well building was attacked by Cromwell's forces in 1650. It was rebuilt in 1889, and the waters were still being used in 1910.

St Margaret's Cave, Dunfermline

Off A994, Chalmers Street car park. (NGR: NT 087873 LR: 65)
The atmospheric cave is associated with Margaret, who used it as a retreat

to worship and pray, and it was a place of pilgrimage. It is reached down
87 steps, and there is a statue in the cave, as well as illustrative panels
about Margaret with an audio guide. The cave is reached through a tunnel
as the ravine in which it was located was filled in for the car park. The
remains of the abbey are nearby.
Explanatory displays. Shop. Car and coach parking.
Open Apr-Sep, daily 11.00-16.00.
Tel: 01383 314228/313838

St Margaret's Chapel, Edinburgh Castle (HS)

Edinburgh Castle, Edinburgh (NGR: NT 252735 LR: 66)
The oldest building in the castle, the small, simple and serene chapel,
dedicated to Margaret, was probably built by David I in the first half of the
12th century, although it is possible it contains older work and Margaret
worshipped here.

It is rectangular in plan with a semi-circular apse, and is whitewashed
inside. The main architectural feature is a fine arch, decorated with zig-
zag patterns or chevrons, between the apse and main body of the chapel.
The chapel had been incorporated into later buildings, and was only

rediscovered in 1845, after which it was restored and the surrounding buildings demolished. It had been used as a powder magazine. A copy of Margaret's gospel is on display here, and there are fine stained-glass windows. There was a larger church within the castle, but this has gone. **See Edinburgh Castle for opening and facilities at the castle.**

St Margaret's Stone, Dunfermline

By A823, 2 miles S of Dunfermline Abbey, 0.5 miles W of Pitreavie, Fife.
(NGR: NT 109850 LR: 65)

The large stone, some eight feet high, is said to mark the resting place of St Margaret on her way to and from Dunfermline. Margaret is said to have received and tried to help ordinary folk here. Her stone was also visited

by women wanting to conceive and ensure a successful birth. It lies near Pitreavie, about half way between Queensferry and Dunfermline.
Access at all reasonable times.

St Margaret's Well, Holyrood Park (HS)

Off A1, 1 mile E of Edinburgh Castle, Holyrood Park, Edinburgh.
(NGR: NT 271737 LR: 66)

St Margaret's Well is located in Holyrood Park, near the track to Hunter's Bog, opposite the Palace of Holyroodhouse. It is housed within a small vaulted building, which is apparently based on St Triduana's Well at

Restalrig. The well building was moved here in 1860 from the present site of St Margaret's House near Meadowbank, then used as railway workshops. The well structure was rebuilt here, and apparently uses the water from St Anthony's Well [NT 275736] (a boulder and stone basin are further up the hill on the track to the ruins of St Anthony's Chapel).

There was probably a royal park from early in the 12th century when nearby Holyrood Abbey was founded by David I (see separate entry). David is said to have been hunting in Holyrood when he was thrown from his horse and attacked by a large stag. A vision of the Cross appeared, and David was saved, so he founded an abbey of Holy Rood (Cross), which he endowed with Margaret's Black Rood of Scotland. The guest house of the abbey was developed into the Palace of Holyroodhouse, which is still used as the official residence of the monarch when in Scotland.

The park is in the centre of Edinburgh and can be reached from various points in the city including a gate beside Holyrood House. There are several small lochs, one of them known as St Margaret's Loch, with many swans and ducks, as well as fine views over Edinburgh and pleasant walks. Arthur's Seat dominates the park, and rises over 800 feet above sea level, and there are prehistoric sites including forts and field terraces.

Plaque. Car parking.

Access at all reasonable times.

Tel: 0131 556 1761/0131 652 8150

Stirling Castle (HS)

Off A872, Upper Castle Hill, in Stirling. (NGR: NS 790940   LR: 57)

One of the most important and powerful castles in Scotland, Stirling Castle stands on a high rock, and consists of a courtyard castle, which dates in part from the 12th century. The castle is entered through the 18th-century outer defences and 16th-century forework of which the Prince's Tower and the gatehouse survive, but the Elphinstone Tower has been reduced to its base. The gatehouse leads to the Lower Square, which is bordered on one side by the King's Old Building, and on another by the gable of the Great Hall.

A road leads between the King's Old Buildings and the hall to the Upper Square. The Chapel Royal is built on one side of the square, as is the Great Hall, which was completed during the reign of James IV. The Chapel Royal was remodelled by James VI in 1594, and James was (earlier!) baptised here. The ceiling and part of the walls were decorated in 1628.

Other features of interest are the kitchens, the wall walk and the nearby 'King's Knot', the earthworks of a magnificent ornamental garden, which once had a pleasure canal.

The earliest recorded castle at Stirling was used by Malcolm Canmore in the 11th century. Alexander I died here in 1124, as did William the Lyon in 1214. Edward I of England captured the castle in 1304, William Wallace took the castle for the Scots, but it was retaken by the English until the

Battle of Bannockburn in 1314. James II was born here in 1430, as was James III in 1451. Mary, Queen of Scots, was crowned in the old chapel in 1543, and the future James VI was baptised here in 1566.

Some of the fine 16th-century town wall of Stirling also survives, and other interesting buildings in the burgh include the Church of the Holy Rude, Argyll's Lodging, Mar's Wark and Cowane's Hospital.

Guided tours are available and can be booked in advance. Exhibition of life in the royal palace, introductory display, medieval kitchen display. Museum of the Argyll and Sutherland Highlanders. Shops. Restaurant. WC. Disabled access and WC. Car and coach parking. Group concessions. £££.

Open all year: Apr-Sep daily 9.30-17.15 (last ticket sold); Oct-Mar daily 9.30-16.15 (last ticket sold); castle closes 45 mins after last ticket sold – joint ticket with Argyll's Lodging; closed 25/26 Dec.

Tel: 01786 450000   Fax: 01786 464678

Urquhart Old Parish Church

Off A96, 4 miles E of Elgin, E side of Urquhart, Moray.
(NGR: NJ 288626   LR: 28)

Nothing remains of the old parish church, dedicated to St Margaret, except the burial ground, which has some interesting memorials.

Access at all reasonable times.

Vikingar!, Largs

Off A78, Greenock Road, Largs, Ayrshire. (NGR: NS 203603   LR: 63)

Vikingar! charts the history of the Vikings in Scotland from the first raids in Scotland to the Battle of Largs in 1263. Displays use mutimedia techniques, including sight, sounds and smells, and are divided into four parts: The Homestead; The Hall of the Gods; The Main Auditorium with an 18-minute video; and The Hall of Knowledge. There is a Viking festival in Largs in late August or early September with features such as the burning of a Viking longboat and a re-enactment of the Battle of Largs. St Margaret is said to have appeared to Scottish troops before the battle, which, although a confused affair, left the Scots victorious.

Guided tours. Multimedia exhibition. Gift shop. Cafe and bar. Swimming pool and play area. WC. Full disabled access. Car and coach parking. Group concessions. ££.

Open all year: Apr-Sep, 10.30-18.00; Oct-Mar, 10.30-16.00.

Tel: 01475 689777   Fax: 01475 689444

Web: www.vikingar.co.uk   Email: info@vikingar.co.uk

Some Other Places of Interest

Other abbeys and priories, many ruinous and some fragmentary, which can be visited include **Beauly Priory** near Inverness, **Cambuskenneth Abbey** (burial place of James III) near Stirling, **Crossraguel Abbey** near Maybole in Ayrshire, **Dundrennan Abbey** near Kirkcudbright, **Glenluce Abbey** in Galloway, **Inchmahome Priory** near Aberfoyle, **Kelso Abbey** in the Borders, **Oronsay Priory** in Argyll, **Paisley Abbey** (burial place of Robert III) near Glasgow, **Pluscarden Abbey** near Elgin (where there is a well dedicated to St Margaret), **Sweetheart Abbey** near Dumfries and **Whithorn Priory** in Galloway.

Fine churches dating from the 12th and 13th centuries which can be visited include **Birnie Kirk** near Elgin in Moray, **Dalmeny Parish Church** near South Queensferry, **St Athernase Church** at Leuchars near St Andrews in Fife, **St Fillan's Church** at Aberdour in Fife, **St Vigean's Church** near Arbroath, **Stobo Kirk** in the Borders and **Symington Parish Church** in Lanarkshire. **Muthill Church** and **St Mary's Church** at Monymusk also had Culdee communities (St Andrews, Loch Leven, Brechin and Abernethy are mentioned above). **Dunkeld Cathedral** (Ethelred, son of Margaret and Malcolm, was Bishop of Dunkeld) and **St John's Kirk** in Perth (burial place of the heart of Alexander III) are also open to the public.

Some magnificent castles also survive (in part) from the 12th and 13th centuries. The largest and most interesting include **Bothwell Castle** near Uddingston in Lanarkshire, **Dirleton Castle** near North Berwick in East Lothian, **Caerlaverock Castle** near Dumfries, and **Kildrummy Castle** in Aberdeenshire. These all saw action in the Wars of Independence. Some motte and bailey castles also survive, including **Coulter Motte** near Biggar, **Druchtag Motte** near Whithorn, **Duffus Castle** near Elgin, and **Motte of Urr** near Dalbeattie.

Sites in England mentioned in the text and open to the public include **Alnwick Castle** and the cross said to mark the spot where Malcolm Canmore was slain, **Bamburgh Castle**, and **Lindisfarne** in Northumbria; **Durham Cathedral** (where the Black Rood of Scotland was taken after being stolen from the Scots at Neville's Cross); and **Carlisle Castle** (David I died here) in Cumbria.

Index

Underlined page numbers refer to an illustration

Page numbers in **bold** refer to the main entry in the places of interest